KEN
Teashop

Other areas covered in the Teashop Walks series include:

The Cotswolds

South Devon & Dartmoor

Dorset

East Anglia

Essex

Hampshire & the New Forest

Lancashire

Lincolnshire

Sussex

Thames Valley

Yorkshire Dales

KENT
Teashop Walks

Jean Patefield

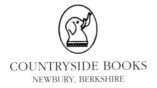

COUNTRYSIDE BOOKS
NEWBURY, BERKSHIRE

COUNTRYSIDE BOOKS
3 Catherine Road
Newbury, Berkshire

To view our complete range of books,
please visit us at
www.countrysidebooks.co.uk

ISBN 1 85306 683 4

Designed by Graham Whiteman
Cover illustration by Colin Doggett
Maps and photographs by the author

Produced through MRM Associates Ltd., Reading
Printed by Woolnough Bookbinding Ltd., Irthlingborough

Contents

Walk

Walk

KEY TO SKETCH MAPS

Path on route	— — →	Teashop	
Path not on route	• • •	Pub referred to in text	PH
Road	═══	Point in text	⑤
River, Stream or canal	∿∿∿∿	Car park	▢
Sea, lake or pond		Building or feature referred to in text	■
Summit	▲	Railway	+++++++
Churches	†		

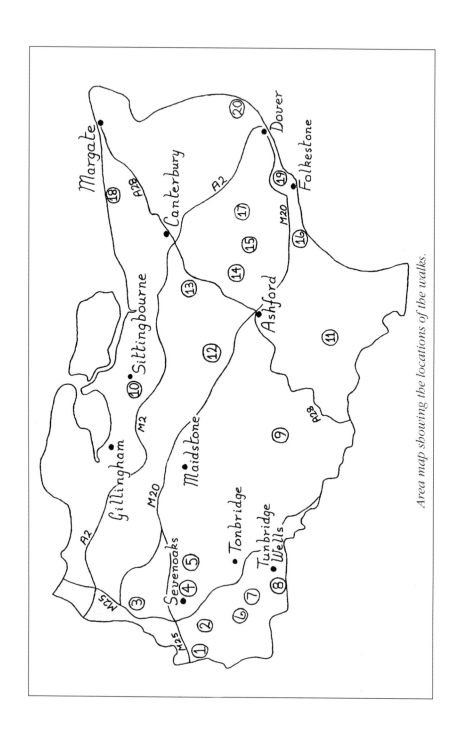

Area map showing the locations of the walks.

Introduction

'Kent, sir – everyone knows Kent – apples, cherries, hops and women', said Dickens through the mouth of Jingle. It is, of course, the garden of England with orchards heavy with fruit in autumn, hop gardens massed with bines, stately avenues of trees and blazing shrubberies in well tended parkland. This is but one face of this large and complex county.

Scenically, Kent is a county of contrasts. The North Downs sweep through the county in a long arc to plunge into the sea as the white cliffs, an enduring image of England. The glorious heights of the Greensand Ridge with their canopy of beech woods and sudden, breathtaking vistas are more dramatic and provide wonderful walking.

Kent has a long coastline, which is in a state of constant change and this adds to the interest of coastal walks. Places that were once important ports, such as Lympne and Appledore, are now quiet backwaters several miles from the sea (see walks 11 and 16). Where once there was a sea-lane so important the Romans built forts at either end to guard it, there is now rich, low-lying agricultural land (see walk 18). The mighty cliffs are prone, in fact, to falling down as the sea batters them. This has given a fascinating jumbled landscape near Folkestone, explored by walk 19.

Kent is also the gateway to England. Caesar landed here and declared it quite civilised! When the Romans returned a century later to settle, the locals were quick to enjoy the benefits, as we see on walk 3. When the Roman legions finally left some four hundred years later, Kent was raided and invaded by Jutes, Saxons and Vikings. William the Conqueror chose to invade through Sussex but soon recognised the importance of Kent and many Norman castles were built.

Throughout English history, Kent has stood in the front line of attack. Napoleon planned to invade here and we can still see the defences erected to oppose him, on walks 11, 16 and 19. A hundred and forty years later Kent again stood in the front line as Hitler planned to invade. Many of the same defences were pressed into action again, alongside new ones. In 1940 the Battle of Britain was fought in the sky over Kent and 'the few' are remembered by the Battle of Britain Memorial, visited on walk 19.

Close to the influence of the capital and the attractions of the rest of Europe, Kent has always attracted the wealthy and influential to make their country homes here, lavishing on them the finest craftsmanship and surrounding them with magnificent parkland. See walks 4, 5 and 6. For the same reasons it has housed the foremost religious seat at Canterbury, which attracted hordes of pilgrims after the murder of Archbishop Thomas à Becket in his cathedral. See walks 12 and 13.

The rich agriculture, advantageous position and trade with Europe were enough to make Kent prosperous but there were also important cloth and iron industries. By the 14th century, Kent was the richest county in England. The social inequalities led to unrest. Wat Tyler led the Peasant's Revolt of 1381 (see walk 11), inspired by the preaching of John Ball, the 'mad priest of Kent'. In 1450 Ashford's Jack Cade led the revolt against the misgovernment of Henry VI, defeating Royal forces at Sevenoaks (see walk 4). In both cases the rebels reached London and were seduced by promises of reform. These were cynically disregarded and the leaders mercilessly hunted down and executed.

Tea is often said to be the best meal to eat out in England and I believe tea is a meal to be enjoyed on all possible occasions. The custom of afternoon tea is said to have been invented by Anna, Duchess of Bedford, in about 1840. She often became peckish in the late afternoon – don't we all? – and invited her friends to join her in a snack of sandwiches and cake. Scones with clotted cream and strawberry jam, delicious home made cakes, toasted teacakes dripping with butter in winter, delicate cucumber sandwiches in summer, all washed down with the cup that cheers, are some of the best, typically English food available and often excellent value. Bad for the figure maybe, but the walking will see to that.

Tea is not only refreshing during a walk; it is good for you! In Scotland apothecaries sold it and it was available on prescription on form number 99. This is the origin of the name of one famous brand. Another, Typhoo, is the Chinese word for doctor

The best teashops serve a range of cakes, all home made and including fruit cake as well as scones and other temptations. Teapots should be capacious and pour properly. Many of the teashops visited on these walks fulfil all these criteria admirably and they all offer a good cup of tea. They always have at least light lunches available as well so there is no need to think of these walks as just something for the afternoons.

There is an abundance of excellent establishments in Kent but even so, tea shops are not scattered evenly throughout the county. In some places popular with tourists, the visitor is spoilt for choice. In such cases the most convenient teashop that, in the author's opinion, most closely fulfils the criteria set out above is recommended but should that not appeal, there are others from which to choose. In some places where there is a delightful walk to be enjoyed, the choice for tea is more limited. However, they all offer a good tea part way round an attractive walk. The opening times and telephone number of each teashop are given. Some are rather vague about when they open out of season: it seems to depend on weather and mood. If you are planning a walk on a wet November Tuesday, for example, a call to check that tea will actually be available that day is a wise precaution. A few are definitely closed in the depths of winter and for these walks, where possible, an alternative source of refreshment is given. In most cases, these are pubs serving food, which in some cases includes tea.

The pleasures of summer walking are obvious. Many of the teashops featured in this book have an attractive garden where tea can be taken outside when the weather is suitable. However, let me urge you not to overlook the pleasures of a good walk in winter. The roads and paths are quieter and what could be better than sitting by an open fire in a cosy teashop scoffing crumpets that you can enjoy with a clear conscience due to the brisk walk to get them!

The 20 walks in this book explore the varied landscapes of Kent. They are all between 3 and 8 miles long and should be well within the capacity of the average person, including those of mature years and families with children. They are intended to take the walker through this attractive corner of England at a gentle pace with plenty of time to stop and stare, to savour the beauty and interest all around. A dedicated yomper and stomper could probably knock off the whole book in a single weekend but in doing so they would have missed the point and seen nothing. To fully appreciate the countryside it is necessary to go slowly with your eyes and ears open.

Some of the walks are short and level, ideal for a pipe opener on a winter's day, or giving plenty of time to dawdle away a summer's afternoon. Others are longer or more strenuous, some making an excellent all day expedition. Certain of the walks involve some climbing. This is inevitable as hills add enormous interest to the countryside and with no hills there are no views. However, this presents no problem to the sensible walker who has three uphill gears – slowly, very slowly and admiring the view. None of the walks in this book are inherently hazardous but sensible care should be taken. Many of the falls that do happen are due to unsuitable footwear, particularly even soles since grass slopes can be as slippery as the more obviously hazardous wet, smooth rock. Proper walking shoes or boots also give some protection to the ankle. It is also essential to look where you are putting your feet to avoid tripping up. Wainwright, the doyen of walkers in the Lake District, said that he never had a serious fall in all his years and thousands of miles of walking because he always looked where he put his feet and stopped if he wanted to admire the scenery.

All the routes are on public rights of way or permissive paths and have been carefully checked but, of course, in the countryside things do change; a stile replaces a gate or a wood is extended. A sketch map illustrates each walk and they are all circular. An Ordnance Survey map is useful as well, especially for identifying the main features of views. The Explorer 1:25,000 (2½ inches to 1 mile) series are by far the best maps to use for walking. Sheets 125, 135, 136, 137, 138, 147, 148, 149 and 150 cover Kent. The grid reference of the starting point and the appropriate maps are given for each walk.

A right of way is exactly what it says – it gives a right of passage over what is otherwise private land. Landowners are not allowed to block a right of way but agricultural activities such as ploughing and harvesting sometimes of necessity, obliterate footpaths and this is legal providing the path is restored within two weeks. Many farmers are conscientious about this and even where they are not, the walkers' feet will do the job on a well used path. Problems can arise when a farmer does not restore a little used path and crops grow up across the line. What is the walker to do? To walk round the edge of the field is technically a trespass and anyway is not always as easy as it sounds. The alternative is to keep to the line of the path and trample down the crops. This is what the law requires you to do, providing no more damage than absolutely necessary is caused, and yet this course of action often doesn't feel right. The solution in each case is a matter of common sense but it is always worth remembering when walking in the countryside that a right of way is not a concession but a prerogative and that footpaths and bridleways are part of this country's highway network.

The walks are designed so that, starting where suggested, the teashop is reached in the second half so a really good appetite for tea can be worked up and then its effects walked off. Some walks start at a car park, which is ideal. Where this is not possible, the suggested starting place will always have somewhere where a few cars can be left without endangering other traffic or causing inconvenience. However, it sometimes fits in better with the plans for the day to start and finish at the teashop and so for each walk there are details of how to do this.

So put on your walking shoes and prepare to be delighted by the charms of Kent and refreshed by a traditional English tea!

Jean Patefield

This is an outstanding walk in the far west of Kent. Much of the outward leg is through woods crowning the hills hereabouts. The paths are well marked and easy to follow and this must be some of the best woodland walking in Southern England. As Westerham is approached, the route leaves the woods and there are magnificent views. The shorter return leg is a refrain, with more views as you climb out of Westerham and there is a final outstanding stretch of woodland. This could have been subtitled 'Winnie's Walk', as the route passes the entrance to Sir Winston's country home, Chartwell, which is open to the public. Tea is taken overlooking The Green in Westerham, which is graced by a statue of Winston Churchill, given by the people of Yugoslavia in recognition of his contribution as war leader in the dark days of the Second World War.

 The Tudor Rose is a traditional teashop with unusual settle seats and a couple of tables outside, overlooking The Green. It prides itself on the quality of its home-cooked food and serves a good selection of delicious cakes. There is a wide choice for lunch from sandwiches through salads and snacks to full meals. These include vegetarian options such as lentil and nut roast. The Tudor Rose is open throughout the year from 8.30 am until 5.30 pm every day except Wednesday. Telephone: 01959 562391.

DISTANCE: 4½ miles.

MAP: OS Explorer 147 Sevenoaks and Tonbridge.

HOW TO GET THERE: The car park where this walk starts is on the east side of the B2026 ¾ mile south of its junction with the A25 at the east end of Westerham. It is a large car park but not well signed.

STARTING POINT: Hosey Hill car park (GR 453531).

ALTERNATIVE STARTING POINT: If you wish to visit the teashop at the beginning or end of your walk, start in Westerham where there is ample parking in a car park signed from the main road. The teashop overlooks The Green. You will then start the walk at point 11.

THE WALK

1. With your back to the road, take a path from the rear right corner of the car park. After 50 yards bear right and follow the main path through the woods.

In the past, woodland was even more of an asset than it is today. It was a valuable source of timber, a source of food from hunting and animals were turned out to graze beneath the trees, On the left of this path are the remains, a ditch and bank, of an ancient structure constructed to mark the boundary between neighbouring owners. On top of the bank are trees. In the past they have been 'laid' to make a hedge so they have grown with multiple trunks.

2. Watch for the ancient boundary turning left, just after a path on the right. After a further 15 yards turn left on a way-marked path then bear right at a fork after a further 25 yards. Continue ahead on the way-marked path over a cross path and ignoring paths to right and left to a surfaced drive.

3. Turn right for 40 yards then left on the second of two adjacent paths, signed 'Greensand Way'. Join a path coming in from the left after 45 yards and continue to a lane. Cross the lane and take the left-hand one of two adjacent paths to continue on the Greensand Way to a second lane.

The entrance to Chartwell is on the left. Today owned by the National Trust, it is a fascinating memorial to the long and chequered life of one of the giants of the 20th century, Winston Churchill. He bought the house in 1922 when he lost both government office and his parliamentary seat with the defeat of the Liberals under Lloyd George. He had originally entered Parliament as a Conservative in 1900 but crossed the floor and joined the Liberals. He returned to Parliament in 1924, again as a Conservative, but, perhaps not surprisingly, was not trusted and spent much of the next 15 years in the political wilderness until he emerged triumphant as war leader. This was his home during those barren years; he referred to Chartwell as an oasis in his political desert. During the war Chartwell was too vulnerable to be the home of the leader but he returned after the war and lived here for the rest of his life. It is too much of a home to let the shrine get the upper hand though several rooms house displays on various aspects of his life. These include a poster from the Boer War offering £25 for his capture, dead or alive. One of the interests with which he occupied himself during his years in the wilderness was bricklaying and he built many of the walls in the garden. In 1928 he sparked an uproar when he took out a card as an adult apprentice in the Amalgamated Union of Building Trade Workers. Chartwell is open Wednesday to Sunday between March and October and Wednesday, Saturday and Sunday in November and December. Telephone: 01732 866368.

4. Go across the second lane and up some steps. Follow the main way-marked path uphill, ignoring paths to the left and a major path joining on the right. Go over a track to a T-junction in front of a wooden fence.

5. Turn right, then bear right after 30 yards down to a road. Cross the road and continue on a track.

6. Some 10 yards after the entrance drive to April Cottage continue ahead when the Greensand Way turns left. The official path is a bridleway and can be unpleasantly muddy. However, you can escape this by using a walker's path on the left that rejoins the track farther on. Eventually, a high wooden fence starts on the right.

7. When the fence ends and the track turns left, go over a stile ahead into a field. Cross the field to a second stile, then continue with a wood on the left to a third stile by a field gate.

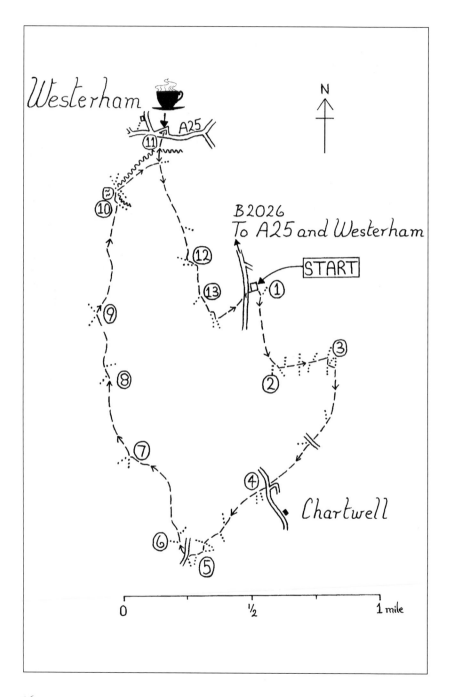

Westerham

A25

B2026
To A25 and Westerham

START

N

Chartwell

0   ½   1 mile

Winston Churchill's statue adorns the village green at Westerham

8. Over the stile, follow a track ahead uphill.

9. As the track starts to descend, watch for a stile on the right, opposite a path. Cross the stile and head slightly left to another stile. Go ahead and the path is shortly fenced and leads to a stile onto a track.

10. Turn left. Opposite a pond on the left, turn right across a bridge over a river and walk along the left-hand side of a field. Watch for a wooden kissing gate on the left. Go through this and follow a surfaced path to The Green in Westerham and the teashop opposite.

Westerham is the most westerly village in Kent, close to the Surrey border. Statues on the picturesque, sloping village green honour the heroes with whom Westerham is associated, James Wolfe and Winston Churchill. Wolfe was born in Westerham in 1727. His family lived at Quebec House, then known as Spiers. He was commissioned into the army at 14, not especially young in those days, and rose rapidly after distinguished service at Culloden, to become a Major-General at 30. His career then stagnated for seven years before he was sent to Canada in 1757 in charge of an expeditionary force to dislodge the French. By a combination of an audacious night-time attack on the Heights of Abraham and poor French military strategy, Wolfe won the battle that made Canada British. Already broken in health, he fell mortally wounded at the moment of victory, dying, it is said, with a smile on his face. Quebec House is along the main road to the left as you leave the teashop. It is a 17th century house with a display of portraits and memorabilia of the family and the Battle of Quebec. Open from April to October on Tuesdays and Sundays between 2 pm and 6 pm. Telephone: 01892 890651.

11. Recross The Green and walk back along the surfaced path, Water Lane, to the wooden kissing gate and take the path ahead, uphill, to another kissing gate. Now bear slightly left to a short, sharp descent and a stile on the left into a wood.

12. Over the stile follow the path ahead to shortly join a track coming in from the right.

13. At a fork bear left on a way-marked path for about 150 yards. Turn left on a way-marked path through a gap in a fence and continue parallel with the path you were on before. At a gate on the right, turn left to emerge on a road. Turn left for about 50 yards to the car park where this walk started.

Walk 2
TOY'S HILL AND IDE HILL

This walk is a gem of beautiful woodland mixed with attractive pastoral scenery and, especially on the outward leg, a succession of viewpoints, all with seats thoughtfully provided the better to enjoy the panorama. If you had visited here in late October 1987 you would have been surrounded by devastation caused by the famous hurricane and we can only marvel at the remarkable powers of recovery of the natural world, as the scene is lovely once more. The return passes through Emmetts with glimpses of the famous garden, the highest in Kent. Though not long, this route is quite energetic enough to justify a good tea and your biggest problem will be deciding where to stop for refreshment with a choice of two excellent possibilities.

Behind the Elan Arts Centre in Ide Hill is an excellent teashop. They offer a particularly tempting selection of cakes including some unusual ones. For example, on my visit there was a delicious orange and elderflower cake. There is also an exceptionally wide and imaginative choice of scones both sweet and savoury – fruit, cheese, apple or ginger

19

and walnut. For lunch, possibilities range from soup, sandwiches, filled jacket potatoes or pie of the day served with a side salad to macaroni cheese or lasagne. In addition to the attractive interior, tea can be enjoyed on a delightful, flower-filled patio. They are open Wednesday through to Sunday between 10 am and 5.30 pm throughout the year except for the six weeks or so immediately after Christmas. Telephone: 01732 750344.

☕ The Stable Tea Room at Emmetts Garden, as you would expect from the name, has tables in what were once loose boxes. There are also some tables outside overlooking yet another spectacular view. National Trust tea rooms can be relied on for a good tea, and this is no exception with an appealing selection of cakes and soup, sandwiches or ploughman's for a light lunch. They are open in April and May every day except Monday and Tuesday and between June and October on Wednesday, Saturday and Sunday between 11.30 am and 4.30 pm. Telephone: 01732 868381.

If you decide to enjoy this excellent walk when both teashops are shut the pub in Ide Hill, the Cock Inn, serves food.

DISTANCE: 3½ miles.
MAP: OS Explorer 147 Sevenoaks and Tonbridge.
HOW TO GET THERE: From the A25 at Brasted 2 miles east of Westerham, take a minor road south opposite the King's Arms, signed 'Brasted Chart 1¼ Toy's Hill 2½', for 2¼ miles to a National Trust car park on the right.
STARTING POINT: Toy's Hill car park (GR 460517).
ALTERNATIVE STARTING POINT: If you wish to visit the teashop at the beginning or end of your walk, start in Ide Hill where there is street parking round the village green. The teashop overlooks the green. You will then start the walk at point 5.

THE WALK

1. With your back to the road, make your way to the left rear corner of the car park and take a path signed 'Octavia Hill's Well' and way-marked as the Greensand Way and National Trust orange route.

Toy's Hill lies on the sandstone ridge that is within the bowl of the North and South Downs and is higher than either at 770 feet above sea level. The National Trust owns over 450 acres of this beautiful area. The woods for which Toy's Hill is famous were devastated in the hurricane of October 1987 and it is very interesting to see how they are regenerating. Some 50 acres have been left entirely untouched so scientists can record the processes of recovery. Most of the fallen trees were cleared out but some were left and this provides an important habitat for fungi and various

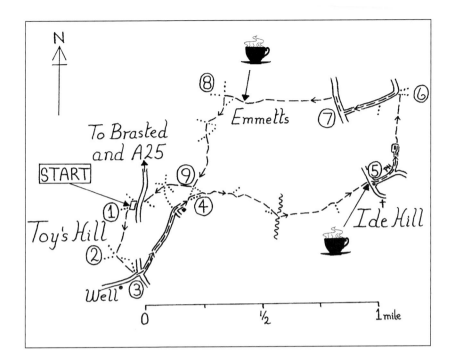

creepy crawlies that feed on the decaying wood. In the past this area was used as wood pasture, a dual-purpose management scheme. The trees were pollarded. This means the branches were cut at head height to provide fuel and wood for small building jobs. The trees have the capacity to sprout new branches and can be cut on a 12 to 15 year rotation. Lopping them at head height keeps the succulent new growth safe from the animals that are allowed to graze the forest floor beneath. Cutting the branches in this way may seem rather brutal but it has the effect of prolonging the tree's life! A beech tree would ordinarily live for about 250 years but pollarding allows the tree to live for 400 years. Few of the pollarded beeches for which the woods were once famous survived the storm. Eventually it is planned to recreate the pollards. This walk makes use of the Greensand Way; a 110-mile long distance path along some of the highest land in Southern England.

2. At a cross path turn left. Take the right fork after 35 yards and follow this path to emerge on Puddledock Lane in the village of Toy's Hill. To visit Octavia Hill's well, turn right first for a couple of hundred yards.

21

Octavia Hill well

Octavia Hill, one of the founders of the National Trust, had this well sunk in 1898 for the people of the village. Previously they had had to collect water from the Puddledock stream and struggle back up a steep hill with their buckets. Even after the well was sunk, water was still precious as it took two people to wind a bucket of water up the 96 feet. This task was made easier when an electric pump was installed in the 1930s. Octavia Hill also gave the terrace on which the well stands to the National Trust and the view south to Ashdown Forest is magnificent.

3. Turn left. Cross a main road and continue in the same direction along Scords Lane. After passing a house called 'Little Chart' this becomes a track. When the surface restarts bear left on a bridleway for 10 yards then take a way-marked path on the right to a T-junction with a cross path.

4. Turn right. Ignore a path on the left and continue to a stile. Over the stile turn left along the top of a field to another stile and Ide Hill church comes into view ahead. Now bear right to a footbridge over a stream then continue along the left-hand side of the first field and the right-hand side of two more to a stile. Continue in the same direction into the village and turn right to the teashop.

5. Cross the road in front of the teashop and go ahead with the village green on the right. At the post office fork left on a minor road to walk in front of the Cock Inn. At the end of the road carry on in the same direction, signed 'Public Footpath to Brook Place'. The path shortly bears right across a field to a stile.

The church overlooking the sloping village green is relatively modern and the highest in Kent. It was built in 1807. Before that the villagers had to walk down to Sundridge and, of course, trudge back up.

6. Over the stile turn left a few yards to a lane and left along the lane to a road.

☕ **7.** Turn right for 180 yards then left on a public footpath along a drive, passing a cricket field. This eventually leads to the tea room through Emmetts Garden. **You must not stray from the public footpath to explore its charms without paying the entrance fee**. Pass to the left of the tea room and continue ahead on a signed path. Ignore a path on the left immediately after a stile and press on for 70 yards to a cross path.

The outdoor eating area at the Stable Tea Room

This superb garden is in the care of the National Trust and open to the public. It dates back to the 1860s but its shrubs and specimen trees were devastated in 1987. The positive side to this devastation was that it gave the opportunity for new planting. Miraculously, a giant Wellingtonia more than a century old survived the storm. It is said to be the highest tree top in Kent. The gardens are open between 11 am and 5.30 pm on Wednesday to Sunday from early April until early June and on Wednesday, Saturday and Sunday for the rest of the summer until the end of October and also Bank Holiday Mondays. Telephone: 01732 868381.

8. Turn left. Carry on across a cross-track as the path bears left and then over a cross path with a wooden barrier to the left.

9. At the next cross path turn right. You are now back on the Greensand Way. At a cross path just before the path climbs steeply turn left. Ignore an immediate path on the left way-marked with red and green arrows and continue ahead to a road and the car park.

Walk 3
DARENT VALLEY

Samuel Palmer, the 19th century artist, called the Darent Valley the 'veil of Heaven'. Only 22 miles from central London, this peaceful landscape seems a world away from the bustling metropolis. The walk starts in Otford, an interesting and ancient village. It wends along quiet field paths and lanes and by the river the 6 miles to Eynsford. On the way it passes through Shoreham, by Lullingstone Castle and an excavated Roman villa. The walking is very easy but do allow plenty of time for this charming ramble because there is so much of interest to see along the way. After a short walk through Eynsford, most of the return is by train so you can briefly enjoy the attractive landscape once more. Please note that the service is about once an hour at the time of writing but is more limited on Sunday afternoon so it is worth checking first so you can organise the day to avoid a long wait.

☕ The Old Ford in Eynsford is ideally positioned overlooking the river. It is housed in a building that dates back to the 1800s and was once a bootlace factory! It has a traditional interior and several tables outside. Cream teas are served and there is a good selection of cakes. Other teatime goodies include crumpets and toasted tea cakes. For a light lunch there are sandwiches or ploughman's and there is an extensive choice of daily specials such as, on my visit, steak and red wine pie or braised lamb chops. They are open from 10 am until 5 pm or later every day throughout the year. Telephone: 01322 861733.

DISTANCE: 6 miles.

MAP: OS Explorer 147 Sevenoaks and Tonbridge.

HOW TO GET THERE: Otford is on the A225, Sevenoaks to Farningham road. The station car park where this walk starts is at the east end of the town and is signed from the A225.

STARTING POINT: Otford Station car park. This is free at weekends but there is a charge during the week (GR 532593).

ALTERNATIVE STARTING POINT: If you wish to visit the teashop at the beginning or end of your walk, start in Eynsford where there is a free public car park behind the Plough Inn. Turn left out of the car park to the teashop. You will then start the walk at point 8.

THE WALK

1. Take an unsigned but surfaced path 60 yards from the entrance to the car park on the right. Ignore a path immediately on the left. The path eventually leads through a churchyard to emerge at a roundabout with a pond in the middle. Cross over the roundabout to The Crown and turn left along the High Street.

There has been a community here since Roman times. Offa, King of Mercia, fought a great battle with the men of Kent somewhere in this vicinity in AD774 and in 1016 Canute battled with marauding Danes; it is said the Darent ran red with the Danes' blood and Danes Hollow is on the map to this day. The site of neither battle has been identified for certain. Otford is on the road to Canterbury and the Archbishops had a palace here, now much reduced. Archbishop Warham, spent vast sums on the building and it rivalled Cardinal Wolsey's Hampton Court in magnificence. Henry VIII stayed here with a retinue of over 4,000 followers on his way to the Field of Cloth of Gold. The King coveted his subjects' fine houses. Ingenious Cranmer tried to suggest it was too small for the King, but at 440 feet long and half as wide, that argument did not sound convincing. So the palace passed into the King's hands in 1537 and, such is the fickleness of monarchs, it was falling into ruin before the end of Elizabeth's reign. The attractive pond in the centre of the roundabout was the village's water supply until quite recent times and is the only pond to be listed as an Ancient Monument!

2. Some 50 yards after The Horns on the right, turn right along a drive, signed 'Darent Valley path'. Continue ahead on a fenced path when the drive ends and when this in turn shortly ends, press on along the left-hand side of a field, ignoring a stile on the left giving access to the river bank. Cross a stile and carry on along the left-hand side of a second field up a small rise. Cross a track and continue ahead, now on the right-hand side of a field. At the end of a field carry on in the same direction along a fenced path across a golf course to a surfaced drive.

3. Turn right for some 300 yards then sharp left on a fenced path, signed 'Footpath to Shoreham' on a stone signpost on the ground. This leads to a cricket pitch. Go across to a metal kissing gate to again walk on a fenced path to a lane.

Ahead and left you can see a cross carved into the hillside. It was made as a memorial to the men who gave their lives in the First World War. Sir Joseph Prestwich, the famous geologist, made his home close by. He amazed local people by telling them to sink a well from the top of the hill and promising them they would meet water at 168 feet – and so they did!

4. Turn left. Ignore the first path on the right and walk through the village, past the pub on the left and church on the right.

Shoreham has known as remarkable a collection of visitors and residents as any English village. John Wesley came every year for 40 years to preach. There were riots in the parish church when he first visited; but later he wrote that Shoreham was, 'the most fruitful place in all the circuit'. The preacher started his days with a sermon at 5am while William Blake, the poet and visionary, sometimes slept close by. He came to visit his friend and disciple Samuel Palmer, who lived at Water House on the banks of the Darent. Vernon Cameron was the son of the vicar of Shoreham. He led the second Livingstone relief expedition, sent out to Africa by the Royal Geographical Society. When they arrived at Tabora, in what is now Tanzania, the great explorer had died. They pushed on across Africa and

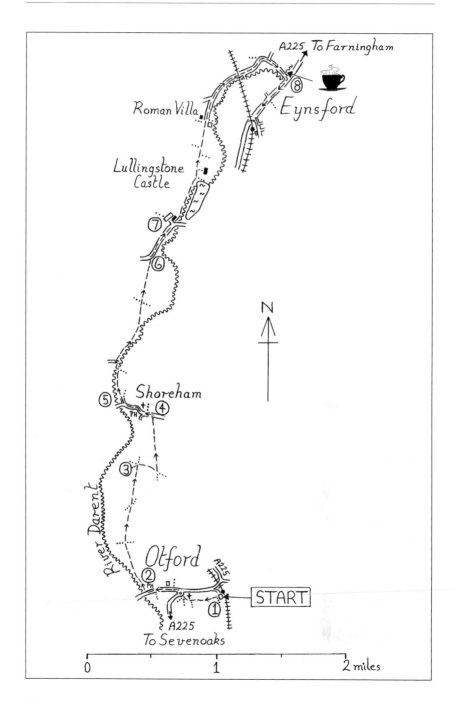

were the first Europeans to cross the continent from sea to sea. Cameron came back in triumph to his village in a train covered in laurels and was met by a band playing 'See The Conquering Hero Comes'.

5. Immediately before a bridge over the river, bear right on the Darent Way then shortly bear left to walk by the river. Cross a footbridge and continue in the same direction on the other side. Join a lane for 20 yards then bear right to carry on by the river. The clear path soon wends away from the river and across fields to a lane. It is easy to follow and well signed.

6. Turn right for about ¼ mile.

7. When the road bends right to a bridge over the river, bear left on a drive to Lullingstone Park Visitor Centre and car park. Almost immediately, turn right on a signed path beside the river. Continue in the same direction past Lullingstone Castle when the path becomes a surfaced drive. Pass the Roman villa and continue along what is now a lane, under a railway viaduct, into Eynsford. The teashop is on the left, just after a bridge and ford across the river.

Relaxing in the garden of The Old Ford teashop

Lullingstone is called a Park because it was enclosed as a deer park in the 13th century. Officially, all deer belonged to the monarch and royal permission had to be granted to establish a deer park for meat and hunting. Lullingstone was sold to the Peche family in the late 14th century and the Castle is still owned by their descendants. It was convenient for the capital and provided good sport. It is not really a castle but a Tudor manor house behind a Queen Anne façade. The family were prominent courtiers throughout the reigns of the Tudors and Stuarts. One was the Chief Sewer (!); he supervised the arrangements of the royal table such as the seating of guests and the tasting of dishes. A later descendant, Sir William Hart Dyke, maintained the tradition of public service. He sat in nine Parliaments, under five speakers, through 13 governments and was one of Disraeli's ministers, living on until 1934. Lullingstone Castle is open to the public at the weekends and on Bank Holidays between May and August. Telephone: 01322 862114.

The landscape we see today is largely a creation of the 18th century when the deer park, which had fallen into disuse, was restored. It was twice threatened in the middle of the 20th century. The demands of death duties meant most of the estate was sold in the 1930s and there were plans to build houses in the Park. Following strong local protests, the local authority bought the Park to protect it as a public open space. There were then plans to construct a new London airport adjacent to the Park to replace fog-prone Croydon. The Second World War intervened and during the war Heathrow was developed so the threat was averted. It was hoped that those flying overhead during the war would think there was an airfield here. It was set up as a decoy for nearby Biggin Hill. Bomber Command created mock buildings and dummy runways, complete with wooden Spitfires and Hurricanes.

Following the Roman Conquest, a farmstead was transformed into a Roman villa. Around AD180 it was taken over by a new owner, who is thought to have been a wealthy Roman of Mediterranean origin who probably worked in Londinium and used the villa as a country retreat. Tiles replaced the thatched roof and elaborate bathing arrangements were installed. The villa was suddenly abandoned about AD200, possibly as a result of the civil unrest in England at that time. It was reoccupied in about AD280 by Romano-Britains. These owners were responsible for the striking mosaics that are such a feature of the site. The owners converted to Christianity towards the end of the fourth century and created a chapel in the villa. It was finally abandoned for good in about AD420. Soil from the hillside above washed down and preserved the site until it was excavated some 1,500 years later. It is now in the care of English Heritage and

The ford at Eynsford

protected by a large hangar. The taped tour is interesting and the site is well worth a visit. Allow about an hour. Open every day until 4.30 pm (4 pm in winter). Telephone: 01322 863467.

8. From the teashop turn right along the main road through Eynsford. Bear left to the station and the train back to Otford.

Eynsford played a part in one of the most turbulent events in English history and was very nearly the home of one of the great inventions of the 20th century. William the Conqueror gave the manor of Eynsfod to one of his courtiers, who called himself de Eynsford. He built a fortified manor house, known as Eynsford Castle. The remains are still to be seen if you turn left instead of right along the main road: they are open every day except Sunday morning. The Archbishop of Canterbury, Thomas à Becket, excommunicated William de Eynsford when he tried to take some feudal benefits from the local priest and William complained to his friend, Henry II. This was one example of the great problem of the age – the balance of power between Church and State. Henry II was provoked to cry, 'Will no one deliver me from this turbulent priest?' and Thomas à Becket was assassinated in his cathedral. William de Eynsford is said to have been filled with remorse at these events and gave up his castle to join the monks.

In 1896 Percy Pilcher was building bamboo gliders in Eynsford. He had considerable success with them, launching off one hilltop and gliding across the valley to land on another. He was convinced that if he could fit an engine and propeller, he would be able to fly. He had tried to find an engine small and light enough, even visiting America in his quest, but had failed to find one. He was designing one himself when he crashed his glider in Leicestershire and was killed. He was 34 years old and a pioneer of flight. Had he lived it is very likely he would have beaten the Wright brothers and been the first man to fly, in which case, Eynsford would have been the cradle of the aeroplane!

Walk 4
KNOLE

This is an outstanding walk through woods and the extensive parkland surrounding Knole House. You are very likely to see herds of deer and, of course, you can combine the walk with a visit to one of England's greatest houses. Managed by the National Trust, this has an excellent tea room. The return traverses more of the park and passes along the top of a steep scarp slope with extensive views south.

The Brewhouse tea room is housed in a 16th century building used for brewing since the 17th century. There are some tables outside in a courtyard. It offers a tempting range of delicious cakes and the cream teas include clotted cream. Light lunches include a ploughman's lunch and a hop-picker's lunch with smoked ham. There is a seasonal soup and a daily special – sausage casserole with cheese and leek mash on my visit. The tea room is open every day except Monday and Tuesday (open Bank Holiday Mondays) between 11 am and 4.30 pm (Sunday until 5 pm) from the beginning of April until the end of October. Telephone: 01732 450608.

When the teashop is closed, there is no other source of refreshment on the route. However, it is not far from Knole House in the centre of Sevenoaks.

DISTANCE: 4 miles.

MAP: OS Explorer 147 Sevenoaks and Tonbridge.

HOW TO GET THERE: On the A25 at Seal east of Sevenoaks, take a minor road, Park Lane, by The Crown. Fork right after 200 yards, signed 'Godden Green Tonbridge', for 2¼ miles to a small car park on the left. This is just after Fawke Wood Road on the right.

STARTING POINT: One Tree Hill car park (GR 558532).

ALTERNATIVE STARTING POINT: If you wish to visit the teashop at the beginning or end of your walk, start at Knole House car park, for which there is a charge. The teashop is signed from the car park. You will then start the walk at point 6.

THE WALK

1. With your back to the road, take a path from the rear left of the car park to shortly reach a broad cross path. Go across this, ducking under wooden horse barriers, and follow the path through the woods to a second cross path.

2. Turn left then fork left after 50 yards. This fork is not very obvious: at the time of writing, there is a fallen tree by the fork and the correct path leads gently downhill to a lane.

3. Turn left and continue past Lower Fawke Farm to a road junction. Go straight ahead, not on the lane but on a signed path to the right of it. Follow this path through woods, across a lane and on through more woods, ignoring a cross path, to a gate through a deer fence into Knole Park. Press on ahead to emerge on a golf course, notified by a sign on a magnificent oak passed on the right. Go ahead to a surfaced drive.

Knole Park has a circumference of about 6 miles and covers some 1,000 acres. You would be very unlucky not to see herds of deer. Deer were once common in the great forests that covered Kent. As the forests were cut down to release land for agriculture, wealthy landowners enclosed tracts of land stocked with deer to provide sport for themselves and their guests and meat for the table. I have seen people feeding the deer in the car park.

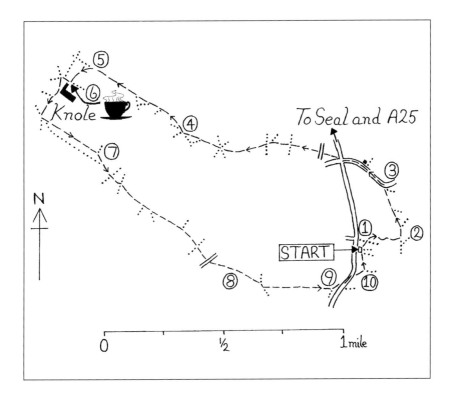

To Seal and A25

START

0   ½   1 mile

N

This is not a good idea because the animals come to associate people with food and lose their fear of humans. If the food is not then forthcoming they can become aggressive and even a danger to small children. The ideal is for the deer to be sufficiently habituated to people so that we can enjoy watching them at quite close quarters but for them to remain relatively timid for their own and our safety.

4. Turn right.

Knole is one of the largest private houses in England and the statistics are quite startling. The roofs cover 4 acres and its design is linked to the calendar with 365 rooms, 12 entrances, 52 staircases and 7 courtyards. Its external appearance is due to Thomas Bourchier, who bought the property in 1456 and transformed it from a medieval jumble to the collegiate structure we see today. In the 16th century Henry VIII coveted both Otford (see walk 3) and Knole, saying that Otford was damp but would do for his retainers but that he would like to live at Knole.

35

Archbishop Cranmer was under no illusions about what was expected and duly handed over the property. Elizabeth I leased and later sold it to her cousin Thomas Sackville and it has remained firmly in the family's hands since. It is now administered by the National Trust but the family still live in part of the house. Vita Sackville-West, who created the garden at Sissinghurst with her husband (see walk 9), was born here. The interior is the work of the Sackville family and has a wealth of paintings, textiles and antiques, including a silver collection dismissed as vulgar by Vita Sackville-West. It is open to the public between Easter and November on Wednesday to Saturday from 11 am until 5 pm and on Sundays from 2 pm until 5 pm.

☕ **5.** Just before the drive descends into a dip cut left across a grassy area to find the entrance to The Brewhouse tea room.

6. Turn left out of the tea room, then left again to the entrance to Knole House. Continue ahead by a wall and follow this round to the left, effectively walking round two sides of a rectangle.

By the middle of the 15th century the people of Kent were in an angry mood. Economic mismanagement, the effects of the Hundred Years War and widespread corruption had undermined their prosperity. There was a series of revolts, not among the peasants who had little to lose, but among the more affluent. These disaffected citizens were organised into a coherent band by Jack Cade, a soldier of fortune with questionable political aspirations. He assembled his forces in Ashford and they marched on London. The royal army tried to stop them south of Sevenoaks, just beyond the boundary of Knole Park to your right. The army overestimated its own capabilities and underestimated those of what they saw as a rebellious rabble. The army was routed in less than an hour and Jack Cade's force marched on to defeat a second royal force at Eltham. Lord Saye and Sele, Lord Lieutenant of Kent, who owned Knole at that time, was a particular focus of their anger and had been put into the Tower for his own protection. He was taken out and his head hacked off by the rebels. Henry VI offered concessions and pardons all round and the force of perhaps 40,000 men went home. The pardon given to their leader was then declared invalid. Jack Cade was killed near Heathfield in Sussex whilst on the run. The wall round the house was built when Jack Cade's rebellion and the fate of Lord Saye and Sele were still fresh in people's memory. It would not deter an all-out assault but is enough to provide some protection as well as privacy.

7. When the wall turns again, go ahead on a path, bearing slightly right to shortly converge with another path. Carry on over a cross path and a surfaced drive, as the path itself becomes a surfaced track. At a surfaced cross track, go ahead to a lane. Cross the lane and continue along a footpath opposite a stile.

8. Over the stile head diagonally right across a field - or round the edge if horsey activities make that advisable - to a stile by a small gate giving onto a cross path. Turn right, then immediately left over a stile onto a fenced path that eventually leads to a drive.

This path is part of the Greensand Way and the views alone would make this walk worthwhile.

9. Turn left a few yards to a lane, then left up the lane for 100 yards.

10. Turn right on a footpath into One Tree Hill Wood. After 110 yards turn left and this path leads back to the start.

Walk 5
OLDBURY WOOD AND IGHTHAM MOTE

This stimulating walk links fifteen hundred years of history. It starts by exploring an Iron Age hill fort, scarcely recognisable beneath its cloak of trees. In addition to the historical aspects of the site, the woods themselves are very interesting, showing how nature is recovering from the devastating storm of 1987. The route then uses quiet tracks and lanes to Ightham Mote, at various times a place of political debate, a stronghold and a stately home and now managed by the National Trust. Be sure to be well refreshed as the return is up and over Raspit Hill, a climb rewarded by delightful woodland walking and extensive, if intermittent, views.

 The Tea Pavilion at Ightham Mote offers the usual excellent National Trust fare. There is a selection of tempting cakes and pastries and scones, with or without cream. For lunch a delicious seasonal soup is served together with sandwiches or a ploughman's. Most of the attractive and unusual octagonal tables are outside but there are some under cover. The Tea Pavilion is open between 11 am and 5 pm every day except Tuesday and Saturday between April and October. Telephone: 01732 811145.

When the teashop is closed, the pub in Ivy Hatch, The Plough, serves food.

DISTANCE: 5 miles.

MAP: OS Explorer 147 Sevenoaks and Tonbridge.

HOW TO GET THERE: From the A25, Sevenoaks to Borough Green road 3 miles east of Sevenoaks, take a minor road signed 'Oldbury Hill' with the National Trust oak leaf symbol. The entrance to the car park is a couple of hundred yards on the left.

STARTING POINT: Oldbury Hill car park (GR 578558).

ALTERNATIVE STARTING POINT: If you wish to visit the teashop at the beginning or end of your walk, start at Ightham Mote car park. The teashop is at the end of the car park. You will then start the walk at point 8.

THE WALK

1. Continue round the loop of the car park until it returns to the lane. Go across the lane to a cross path and turn left. Follow the main path ahead, ignoring many paths to the right. When the path forks, bear left to almost touch the road at Oldbury Hill camp site and press on along the path to a T-junction with a cross track.

Two thousand years ago this spot would have been very different. Instead of a wooded hill to the right there was a bare hillside crowned with earth ramparts and a strong wooden palisade. From the ramparts there must have been commanding views over the surrounding countryside. Hardly recognisable today beneath its cloak of trees, this was one of the most significant Iron Age hill forts on a major trading route. The track you are about to follow was the main road from Seal to Ightham – the A25 of its day!

2. Turn right and follow the track uphill. At a three-way fork by a National Trust notice board, which explains the structure of the ramparts, take the central branch.

You are now walking through the fort, which was built between 150 and 50 BC and covered about 124 acres. The ramparts had a circumference of about 2½ miles. It was not really the military structure its name suggests. In times of peace it served as an administrative and commercial centre

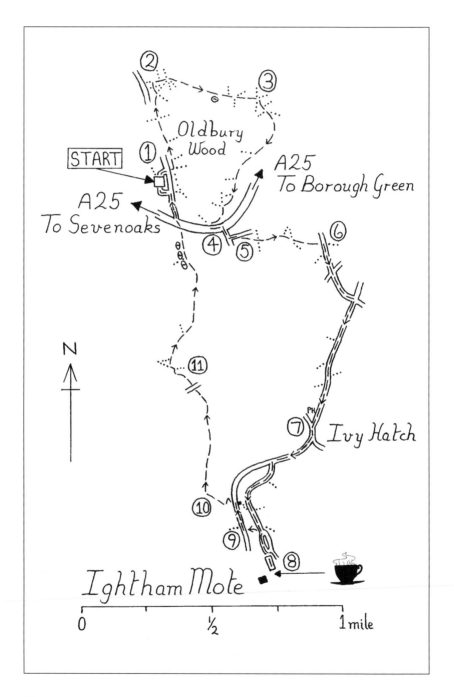

but most people lived on farms in the surrounding countryside. There was a flourishing iron industry in this part of Kent too. In times of trouble it was a defensive position to which people could retreat with their cattle.

3. At the next junction, just before the track starts to go steeply downhill, take the second of two paths on the right - not the signed bridleway. Stay on this path, ignoring all side turns as far as a wooden horse barrier and an obvious cross track. Turn left, downhill, to reach the A25.

This was the southern entrance to the fort. The entry was the most vulnerable part of the fort and was protected by a double gate system. The ramparts are most obvious here.

4. Turn left for 85 yards; fortunately there is a footway. Turn right along Coach Road, signed 'Ivy Hatch 1', then immediately left on Copt Hall Road for 60 yards.

5. Bear right on a signed bridleway. Follow this across several paths and drives to a lane.

6. Turn right. Turn right again at a second crossroad, Ismays Road.

☕ **7.** At a T-junction in Ivy Hatch turn left for 50 yards then right along Mote Road, signed 'Hildenborough 3¾ Ightham Mote ¾' for 300 yards to the entrance to Ightham Mote on the left. Follow the entrance drive to the car park and the tea pavilion beyond.

One of Britain's best medieval manor houses, Ightham Mote lies deep in the countryside some 2 miles south of the village from which it takes its name. It is said that during the Civil War Roundhead troops sent to root out this Royalist refuge got hopelessly lost and never did manage to find the house. Peaceful today, Ightham Mote seems a single, harmonious building in the form of a hollow square surrounded by its moat but its construction spans three centuries from the Cawnes in the 14th century to the Selbys in the 17th. In earlier times this was the site of a Saxon 'moot' or parliament and the name probably derives from this rather than the moat. The most famous member of the Selby family was Dame Dorothy, who was a lady in waiting to Elizabeth I and famed for her fine needlework. It is said that she was instrumental in foiling the Gunpowder Plot. Apparently she wrote anonymously to her cousin, Lord Mounteagle, warning him to stay away from the Opening of Parliament in 1605. He recognised his relation's handwriting and instituted the enquiries that led to the plot being discovered. The National Trust now owns Ightham Mote and it is open to the public from April until October between noon and 5.30 pm. Telephone: 01732 811145.

8. Return through the car park and along the exit drive to where it meets the entrance drive. Take a path on the left, signed with a green arrow, that shortly leads down steps and to a gate onto a lane.

9. Turn right.

10. Opposite Mote Hill Cottage take a signed bridleway on the left into woodland. Follow this uphill, across a lane and on steeply uphill.

11. At the top of the hill, at a T-junction with a cross path, turn left to continue to walk with a wire fence on the left. After 70 yards turn right on a path that leads steeply downhill and on through lovely woods to the A25. Cross the road to take Styants Bottom Road back to the car park.

Walk 6
VICEROY'S WOOD AND CHIDDINGSTONE

This is a most interesting walk for any time of year. Perhaps three-quarters of the route follows woodland tracks. These are interspersed with field paths, which allow attractive views across the Wealden countryside to be enjoyed. The objective of the walk is the village of Chiddingstone, which boasts one of the best preserved and most attractive village streets in England, not to mention an excellent teashop (and pub!). It is worth allowing extra time to explore the ancient church and visit the Chiding Stone, from which the village derives its name.

 The Village Tea Shop in Chiddingstone is part of Burghesh Court, owned at one time by the family of Ann Boleyn, the second wife of Henry VIII. The buildings date back to at least 1453. This is a charming traditional teashop with comfortable chairs and tables outside, some with welcome shade in the summer from a gazebo. There is an excellent range

43

of cakes on offer and cream teas feature clotted cream imported from Totnes. Both light lunches, such as sandwiches and ploughman's, and full meals are served. There is a tempting selection of traditional puddings including treacle tart and bread and butter pudding to send you on your way replete. It is open every day except Monday from 10.30 am until 5 pm between April and November and at weekends in winter. Telephone: 01892 870326.

When the teashop is closed, the pub in Chiddingstone, the Castle Inn, serves excellent food. In addition, refreshments, including a welcome cup of tea, are available by the car park where this walk starts.

DISTANCE: 5 miles.
MAP: OS Explorer 147 Sevenoaks and Tonbridge.
HOW TO GET THERE: From the B2188, the Penshurst to Fordcombe road, half a mile south of Penshurst take a minor road west, signed 'Chidd, Hoath, Chiddingstone, Edenbridge'. Follow the road for about three-quarters of a mile to a track on the left signed 'PORC Penshurst Off Road Cycling'. The track leads up to a car park.
STARTING POINT: PORC (Penshurst Off Road Cycling) car park. This is privately owned but the owner is happy for walkers to use it (GR 513426). On the very rare occasions it is full, there are one or two spots on the lane near the start where it is possible to pull off the road.
ALTERNATIVE STARTING POINT: If you wish to visit the teashop at the beginning or end of your walk, start in Chiddingstone where there is some street parking. The teashop is opposite the church. You will then start the walk at point 10.

THE WALK

Viceroy's Wood has been a playground for centuries. During the 1800s it belonged to the Governor General of India and invited guests would parade, picnic and watch horse racing. Now mountain bikes have replaced the horses. Just by the car park is a huge sweet chestnut, easily recognisable by its deeply fissured bark. It is called the Seven Sisters because of the seven trunks that have developed.

1. Return to the road. Turn left for about 300 yards to a cross path.

2. Turn right, initially down some steps, then follow a path just inside a wood to a stile into a field. Continue ahead across two fields to a stile onto a footbridge. Go ahead to another stile, this time onto a double footbridge. Over the bridges, follow the path,

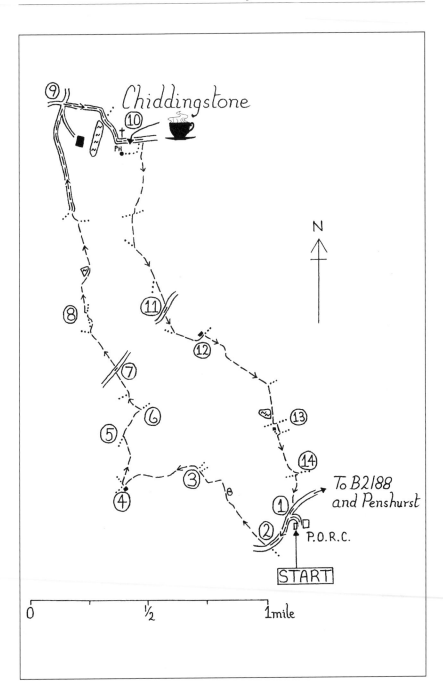

Chiddingstone

N

To B2188
and Penshurst

P.O.R.C.

START

0   ½   1mile

shortly passing a pond on the right. Continue round the left-hand side of a vineyard then follow the path into woodland, shortly crossing another footbridge.

3. Continue ahead as a path joins from the right opposite a metal gate on the left. Ignore another path on the right after some 20 yards and follow the main path round to the left to a stile out of the wood. Go ahead to the left of a line of trees to a stile on the right onto a hedged path. This shortly becomes a track. Walk along the track as far as a half-timbered house on the left.

4. Opposite the house, turn right on a way-marked path; after a few yards this leads to a stile into a field. Over the stile, head right across the field to a stile in the far right corner. Over this continue ahead along the right-hand side of a field to a stile into a wood. Follow a faint path through the trees for 35 yards to a T-junction with a larger cross path.

5. Turn right. Walk through the wood for about 250 yards to a path on the left opposite a metal gate on the right.

6. Turn left. Follow the path through the wood and continue as it becomes a track leading to a lane.

7. Turn right for 35 yards then turn left over a stile on a signed path. Walk down the left-hand side of a field to a stile into a wood. Ignore paths on the left as the main path bears right and follow the path through the wood to a small metal gate into a field. Do not go through the gate but go left inside the wood for 10 yards to a stile into a different field.

8. Over the stile, go ahead with a hedge on the right. When this ends, bear slightly right onto a rough track, shortly passing a large pond on the left. Carry on as the track is first surfaced and then becomes a lane. This leads past the entrance to Chiddingstone Castle to a crossroads.

Chiddingstone Castle, which may be glimpsed from the road, was once known as High Street House and the road ran past it. The Streatfield family were squires of Chiddingstone for 450 years. In the early 19th century, the family fancied something rather more splendid than a mere red-brick house and remodelled the building in the fashionable Gothic style, complete with battlements. The road was diverted to keep the hoi poloi at bay and a lake created, passed on the right. By the 1930s, the Streatfields could no longer afford this miniature stately home and sold up. During the 1940s the building suffered much from military and scholastic occupation and by 1955 it was derelict. It gained a new lease of life as the home of Denys Bower, an art dealer and collector, who built up an eclectic collection ranging from Regency furniture to Egyptian tomb objects and arguably the greatest private collection of Japanese artefacts in Britain. He left it to the National Trust but they refused the bequest. A private charitable trust was set up to run the property, which they have done with help from English Heritage. It is open to the public on Sundays and public holidays between April and September from 11.30 am until 5.30 pm and on Wednesday, Thursday and Friday afternoons between 2 pm and 5.30 pm from June to September. Telephone: 01892 870347.

☕ **9.** Turn right, signed 'Chiddingstone ¼ Leigh 4¾", into Chiddingstone and the tea shop is on the right, opposite the church.

Chiddingstone is a particularly attractive village and is kept that way because the National Trust has owned it since 1939. Its character is wholly Kentish, with half-timbered, tile-hung, buildings overlooking the street. What is now the Castle Inn was mentioned in 17th century documents but is probably a century or two older than that. It first became an inn in 1730 when it was called the Five Bells. The present church, which dates from the 14th century, is the third or fourth building on the site. There is more information available from the guidebook and it is worth a visit for the 'vinegar' bible and stained glass to commemorate the Millennium.

10. From the teashop turn right along the lane.

To visit the Chiding Stone, take a signed footpath on the right just after the school then return the same way to the lane.

The Chiding Stone is an outcrop of sandstone which may variously have been a Saxon boundary stone, a Druid altar and a place where grievances were aired. It is said that nagging and slatternly wives were often publicly 'chided'. I wonder if drunken and straying husbands received the same public warnings.

Some 50 yards after the path to the Chiding Stone, turn right onto a fenced path starting through a metal kissing gate. Follow the clear path ahead through woods and across fields, going over a cross path at a stile. When the path forks after a good half mile, bear left, way marked as the Eden Valley Walk.

11. At a lane turn right for 40 yards then left on a signed path. After a few yards go through a metal gate then across a field to a small metal gate beside a metal field gate and on to a surfaced track. Turn left.

12. Opposite the first farm building on the left, take a track on the right.

13. Pass a pond on the right then immediately after the surfaced track makes a sharp left turn in front of an imposing house, turn right between wooden posts onto a wide path. This leads round the house and garden to a track. Turn left along the track.

14. Watch for a track joining from the right. Turn right along it for 10 yards, almost back on yourself, then turn left on a footpath that climbs through woods to a lane. Turn right for 90 yards to the track up to the car park.

Walk 7
LEIGH AND PENSHURST

Set in a bowl of green hills, Penshurst Place is one of the oldest and greatest of England's country houses. It has a secure place in history as a resort of royalty from when Edward the Black Prince and his Fair Maid of Kent feasted in its Great Hall and Elizabeth I danced with Dudley. Surrounded by formal gardens, it lies on the edge of parkland adorned with graceful avenues of trees. As well as providing an opportunity to visit Penshurst Place, this walk explores the villages of Penshurst and Leigh with their attractive cottages of mellow brick and half timbering. The route passes through a rolling landscape of woodlands, meadows and parkland and the walker is rewarded with some excellent views.

 Quaintways Tearooms are housed in a 16th century building. With a wealth of exposed beams, the rear room is a converted bakehouse and still has its Victorian oven. There is a suntrap garden at the rear. Cream teas are served and for more spartan souls, a plain tea is also offered, without the cream. There was also a good selection of cakes, such as cherry strudel on my visit. Sandwiches and ploughman's lunches with Cheddar, Stilton or pate are available for lunch as well as things on toast. There is a wide selection of teas including fruit and herbal varieties. It is open every day except Monday between 10 am and 5 pm throughout the year. Telephone: 01892 870272.

DISTANCE: 5½ miles.
MAP: OS Explorer 147 Sevenoaks and Tonbridge.
HOW TO GET THERE: Leigh is on the B2027, Tonbridge to Edenbridge road about 4 miles west of Tonbridge. Note: the B2027 is not directly accessible from the A21.
STARTING POINT: Leigh village green (GR 550464).
ALTERNATIVE STARTING POINT: If you wish to visit the teashop at the beginning or end of your walk, start in Penshurst where there is a large lay-by on the B2176 at the northern edge of the village. You will then start the walk at point 8.

THE WALK
1. Walk round the Green to the cricket pavilion and turn down Green View Avenue. At the end go through a wooden kissing gate and follow a path under a railway arch. When the fenced path ends, continue ahead across two fields to a footbridge over the river Medway and on to a second footbridge and a substantial cross path.

2. Go ahead over the cross path to a stile by a field gate. Cut across the end of a field to a second stile, then press ahead along the right-hand side of a large field to a stile on the right by a field gate. Cross the stile onto a gravel track and turn left to continue in the same direction to a lane.

3. Turn right over the river, then left on a signed path to walk by the river for about ¼ mile.

4. Watch for yellow way-marks showing the line of the path, bearing right away from the river to a footbridge over a ditch. Follow the path, marked by posts, uphill to a stile onto a concrete track.

5. Turn right, then immediately left at a T-junction.

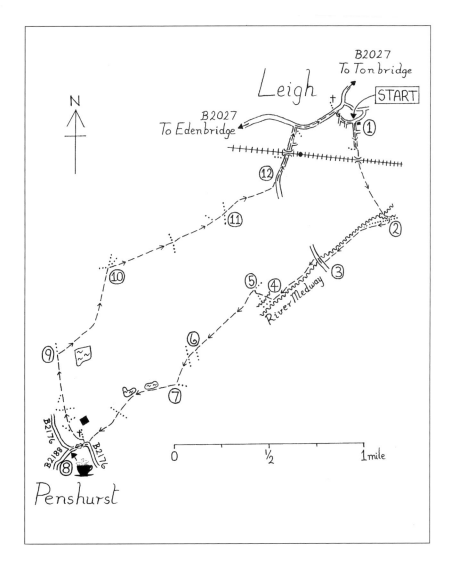

6. When the track bends left, continue ahead through a gate then along the left-hand side of a field to a stile. Now bear slightly left to rejoin the concrete track.

Ahead is an excellent view of Penshurst Place. It was originally built in 1341 as a manor house for the wealthy London merchant Sir John de Poultney, four times Lord Mayor of London, and has been extended and altered many times since. In 1552 Edward VI gave Penshurst Place to his courtier Sir William Sidney and it has been owned by the descendants of the family ever since. Sir Philip Sidney, writing in the middle of the 16th century when the core of the building was already old, referred to it as, 'handsome without curiosity and homely without loathsomeness'. The Great Hall is over 60 feet long and nearly 40 feet wide and, apart from blocking up the central roof vent that carried smoke from the open hearth, has hardly been altered since the 14th century. The massive beams are supported by grotesque carved figures – the peasants on whom the whole social structure ultimately rested. Penshurst Place is open daily from the beginning of April to the end of October and weekends in March. The house is open between noon and 5.30 pm and the gardens from 10.30 am until 6 pm. Telephone: 01892 870866.

☕ **7.** Turn right along the track to a gatehouse and a road. Turn right along the road into Penshurst and the teashop is on the left, almost opposite a road on the right.

8. Turn right out of the teashop and retrace your steps towards the gatehouse. Turn left up some steps and pass between buildings into the churchyard. Pass to the left of the church and over a stile to walk in front of Penshurst Place. At the end of the building, go ahead across a fenced drive. Keep ahead past a cricket pitch and a large oak to a stile.

The entrance to the church is through a group of Tudor and 19th century cottages forming a three-sided courtyard. It is called Leicester Square, after Robert Sidney, Earl of Leicester who was a favourite of Elizabeth I. Its namesake, the more famous Leicester Square in London, was named after the second earl, who built a mansion there in 1631. The church has several interesting features, described in the guide book to be found within.

The Sidneys have been an energetic and influential family. Henry Sidney, son of the statesman to whom Edward VI granted the property, held a strange assortment of court offices including Chief Cupbearer, Otter Hunter and Chief Cypherer. He served as Ambassador to France for the boy King Edward VI and managed to stay in favour during the turbulent years of Mary's reign. He went on to serve as Elizabeth I's Lord Deputy in Ireland. This duty so wore him out physically and financially that by the time he was 54, he described himself as 'toothless and trembling' and he died soon after. His son, Philip Sidney, was a famous poet and soldier. His death is a classic tale of fruitless heroism and the waste of war. A bullet at the Battle of Zutphen in Holland shattered his thigh. He was brought a drink of water to relieve his thirst but gave it instead to a wounded soldier with the words, 'Thy necessity is greater than mine'. He lingered for a few weeks at Arnhem before fatal gangrene set in.

9. Over the stile bear right to a second stile. Over this stile bear left to walk uphill along an avenue of trees, crossing a third stile.

10. At the top of the hill turn right, still walking along an avenue of trees, for a good ½ mile.

11. At the end of the avenue of trees, cross a stile by a gate. Do not mistake this for a stile by a gate part way along the avenue. Bear slightly left across a field to a stile beside a gate into woodland. Follow a track downhill to a road.

12. Turn left into Leigh. Turn right at the main road back to The Green.

Leigh, pronounced Lye, has many Victorian half-timbered houses, including two attractive groups of almshouse-like cottages built by Samuel Morley, a 19th century Nottingham hosier and philanthropist. The church is on a rise overlooking the excellent village green. Inside on the north wall is an unusual Tudor brass which appears to show a woman rising from her coffin, leaving her shroud behind, with the inscription, 'Behold O Lord I com willingly'.

Walk 8
GROOMBRIDGE AND ROYAL TUNBRIDGE WELLS

Starting a couple of hundred yards into Sussex, this beautiful Wealden walk soon crosses into Kent. It basically follows the valley of the river Grom. Almost entirely on most attractive meadow and woodland paths, the route takes the walker into the heart of Royal Tunbridge Wells only a few yards from the historic Pantiles, where there are several tea shops and restaurants. The return leg is mainly in Sussex but involves little walking as it is accomplished by steam train, courtesy of the Spa Valley Railway. Do allow plenty of time for this walk. The route passes Groombridge Place, which has beautiful gardens open to the public. There is much to explore in Tunbridge Wells, including A Day at the Wells. This exhibition, by the same people who created the Jorvik Viking Centre in York and the Canterbury Tales exhibition, recreates the spa town in 1740, complete with sights, sounds and even smells! You may also want to take the waters as well as tea.

The steam trains for the return from Tunbridge Wells run every weekend except in February and November and through the week during the school holidays. Timetable information is available on 01892 537715 or the railways web site, www.spavalleyrailway.co.uk. If the trains are not running on the day you choose to do this walk, at the time of writing there is a bus service on Monday to Saturday from Tunbridge Wells to Groombridge, leaving from the mainline station in Tunbridge Wells.

☕ There is a wide choice of places to eat in The Pantiles, including several teashops. The Garden Coffee Shop in the Corn Exchange makes good use of its position with an attractive conservatory design. In addition to tea and coffee, they serve a tempting hot chocolate with whipped cream. A selection of cakes, gateaux and pastries are offered as well as cream teas. For lunch there are sandwiches and filled jacket potatoes and you can always have 'brea' by combining the all-day breakfast with tea! The Garden Coffee Shop is open every day throughout the year between 9 am on weekdays, and 10 am on Sunday, until 5 pm. Telephone: 01892 544119.

DISTANCE: 4 miles.

MAP: OS Explorer 135 Ashdown Forest.

HOW TO GET THERE: From the A264, Tunbridge Wells East Grinstead road, 3 miles west of Tunbridge Wells, take the B2110 to Groombridge. Bear left off the main road at the Victoria public house into the village centre and the car park beside the village hall.

STARTING POINT: Groombridge village car park (GR 551373).

ALTERNATIVE STARTING POINT: If you wish to visit the teashop at the beginning or end of your walk, start in Tunbridge Wells where there is ample parking in several car parks, notably The Pantiles car park on Major York's Road. The teashop is in the Corn Exchange in The Pantiles. You will then start the walk at point 10.

The walk

1. Go through a gap in the fence at the rear of the car park and turn right. Walk along the left-hand side of an open area to pick up a path that leads to a track. This is part of the High Weald Walk and much of the route to Tunbridge Wells uses this. It is well way-marked and easy to follow.

Groombridge Place is surrounded by delightful gardens, which are open to the public from the end of March until the end of October. Telephone:

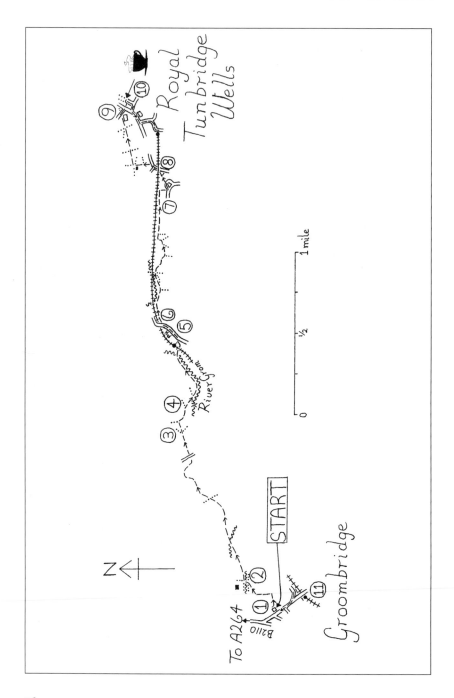

01892 863999. The moated house was built on the site of a Norman castle. The story goes that the owner at the time of Agincourt found the half-brother of the King of France, the Duke of Orleans, lying wounded on the battlefield. He is said to have brought him to Groombridge and nursed him back to health before demanding a ransom from his relations. The King is said to have learned of this and claimed the prisoner and the huge ransom that was eventually paid. The true story is less dramatic. The younger brother of the Duke was handed over as a political hostage three years before the Battle of Agincourt. He was given into the safe keeping of the then owner of Groombridge Place, Sir Richard Waller, who held him here as well as in London and near Peterborough until he was ransomed in 1442. Charles Packer, Clerk to the Privy Seal, erected the present building in 1618. After 1734 the house lay empty for 20 years and may have been used as a smugglers' hideout by the notorious Groombridge Gang during this time.

2. Turn right to shortly cross a bridge and meet a surfaced drive. Turn right again and after a few yards, immediately before a gate across the drive, turn right yet again on a signed path. Follow the path along the left-hand side of several fields. Cross a farm track and continue on a fenced path that eventually leads to a lane. Cross the lane and carry on in the same direction on a track.

3. When this track ends at a cross track, go ahead across a field to a bridge. Go through a field gate then bear right after a further 10 yards on a fenced path leading to a stile.

4. Over the stile, bear left – neither along a fence nor down to a bridge but to walk with young trees on the left. Cross a stile by a huge, old oak. Bear right when the path forks after a few yards and follow the path through meadow and woods. Continue as it leads under a railway bridge and up to a lane at High Rocks Halt.

(If you wish, you can cut the walk short at this point and take the train back to Groombridge or into Tunbridge Wells.)

5. Turn left past High Rocks Inn.

The High Rocks are a series of sandstone outcrops that have been weathered into fantastical shapes. An entrance fee is charged to wander between them but you can see them quite well from the path and some lie outside the private ground.

The High Rocks

6. Immediately before a bridge over the railway, bear right on a path. When the path forks, take the left-hand branch to stay by the river. At the next fork bear left over a stile. Ignore a path on the right then, after a further 30 yards, turn left. There are many paths in this woodland; the correct path is way-marked by yellow arrows.

7. Go through a gate and continue ahead past some lock-up garages. Turn right up to a road. Turn left then bear left to a gap between shops and on to a road.

Tunbridge Wells is famous as a spa town and perhaps as a symbol of outraged gentility but it also has an important place in the history of the motor car. In 1894 the Mayor of Tunbridge Wells Sir David Salomons was very keen on the new horseless carriages. He organised a public exhibition of vehicles on the show ground of the Tunbridge Wells Agricultural Society, which was then just near here. It attracted crowds of thousands to inspect the new phenomenon. During the afternoon he drove his car out of the show ground and along the road. This doesn't sound very startling but as a magistrate he was deliberately flouting the Locomotives and Highways Act, the infamous Red Flag Act that required a man to walk in front of a car with a red flag. The act was repealed in 1896 and was celebrated with a run from London to Brighton, which survives to this day.

8. Turn left, under the railway. Some 50 yards after the bridge, turn left on a signed and surfaced path and follow this uphill. At the end of a house on the left, turn right on the second of two adjacent paths. Follow this ahead to join a surfaced path and on past a car park to a road.

This attractive spa town grew up among the Wealden forests after Lord North discovered its chalybeate spring in 1606. Until then, there were only a few scattered farms and hamlets so Tunbridge Wells has no medieval or Tudor buildings. To begin with, visitors who came to take the waters roughed it in nearby cottages or, like Queen Henrietta Maria, camped out on the common. Building began in 1638 when a grassy promenade called the Walk was laid out beside the spring. Visitors took the waters in the morning and socialised afterwards. Later, the walk was paved with square earthenware tiles, giving rise to its present name, The Pantiles.

9. Cross the road and turn right to a roundabout. Cross a road and go down Swan Passage to The Pantiles. The Corn Exchange and its teashop are slightly to the left down more steps.

In those days Tunbridge Wells was really quite raffish. The waters were supposed to be good for the ailments caused by too much dissipation at court. In the morning people would imbibe their daily dose then sally forth in all their finery to enjoy the entertainments that the town had to offer. The waters were also said to be good for treating infertility in women and many came to help them conceive. It is true that many did become pregnant but whether this was the effect of the water or the many attractive young men who were part of the social scene I couldn't say. You can still take the waters today from the spring in the portico of the Bath House. Traditionally, the water is free but you pay for the services of the Dipper, the woman who collects it for you in a clean glass. It is worth wandering along The Pantiles before continuing the walk. Beau Nash, arbiter of fashion, presided over balls and gambling at the Assembly Rooms, number 40/46. The Corn Exchange was originally built as a theatre and now houses shops, tea rooms and the Day at the Wells exhibition, open throughout the year. Telephone: 01892 546545.

10. Turn left out of the Corn Exchange and walk to the end of The Pantiles. Turn right back to the main road then turn left along it.

Transport for the return leg of the journey!

Turn left along Nevill Terrace to The Old West Station. This is now a restaurant. Trains back to Groombridge and the ticket office are to the right.

The London, Brighton and South Coast Railway built the line in 1866. Like so many branch lines it fell prey to competition from the car and finally closed in 1985. A half mile stretch was reopened in 1996 and the service extended to Groombridge in 1997.

11. At Groombridge Station turn right off the train and walk to the end of the platform, past the original station buildings. Go through a gate and walk down the road ahead. Turn right at a T-junction, back to the car park.

Groombridge is a divided village, lying partly in Kent and partly in Sussex. The old village, across the river, is in Kent and the newer part in Sussex grew when the railway came.

Walk 9
FRITTENDEN AND SISSINGHURST

In the 'garden of England' is one of the great gardens – Sissinghurst. This undemanding route explores the well-kept countryside in the vicinity and approaches the gardens from an unusual direction. The landmark tower is in sight for much of the outward route, acting like a beacon drawing you to tea! The walk is mainly on field paths with short stretches along quiet lanes and you are unlikely to meet many others until close to Sissinghurst.

 The Granary Restaurant is housed in a restored granary and pleasingly combines ancient and modern. It offers the usual excellent National Trust tea with a wide selection of cakes. This includes familiar favourites such as coffee and walnut cake and less usual temptations such as, on my visit, courgette tea bread and chocolate stout cake. As well as the refreshing National Trust tearoom blend of tea, there is a good range of cold drinks including apple juice from local orchards, particularly welcome on a hot summer's day. For lunch the emphasis is on Kentish fare with traditional casseroles and pies making use of as much local produce as possible. Lighter options such as salads and ploughman's are also served. It is open from 11 am until 5.30 pm on Tuesday to Friday and 10.30 am until 5.30 pm at the weekend between the beginning of April and the middle of October. From the middle of October until mid December Sissinghurst is also closed on Tuesday. Telephone: 01580 713097.

When the teashop is closed, there is no other refreshment on the route but there are pubs in Frittenden.

DISTANCE: 4½ miles.

MAP: OS Explorer 137 Ashford, Headcorn, Chilham and Wye.

HOW TO GET THERE: From the A274, Tenterden to Maidstone road, at Bounds Cross chapel 2 miles north of Biddenden, take a minor road signed 'Frittenden 3' for 1 mile. Turn right, signed 'Frittenden 1¼ Staplehurst 5'. At a T-junction in Frittenden turn left, signed 'Sissinghurst 3 Cranbrook 4 Hawkhurst 8' to the church on the right and Memorial Hall on the left. Park near the Memorial Hall.

STARTING POINT: Frittenden Memorial Hall (GR 813408).

ALTERNATIVE STARTING POINT: If you wish to visit the teashop at the beginning or end of your walk, there is a large National Trust car park at Sissinghurst for people visiting the gardens. The teashop is signed from the car park. You will then start the walk at point 7.

THE WALK

The road you drove along to start this walk was once followed by swine driven to pasture in the dense oak woods of the Weald. Frittenden grew up along this ancient drove route and was first mentioned in a charter of AD804. A quiet backwater in history, a church has stood here from at least the 11th century and probably before. By the 19th century it had fallen into decay when a wealthy and energetic rector, Edward Moore, rebuilt it almost entirely at his own expense. Nearly everything the visitor sees dates from this time. When the work was completed, Reverend Moore crowned his achievement by paying for a feast of roast beef and plum pudding for over 1,000 guests who were entertained by a brass band and glee singers. Not surprisingly, a prominent memorial in the churchyard remembers this benefactor.

1. With your back to the road, take a signed path to the right of the Memorial Hall. This shortly leads across two fields. Continue ahead for 150 yards across a third field to a post where the path branches.

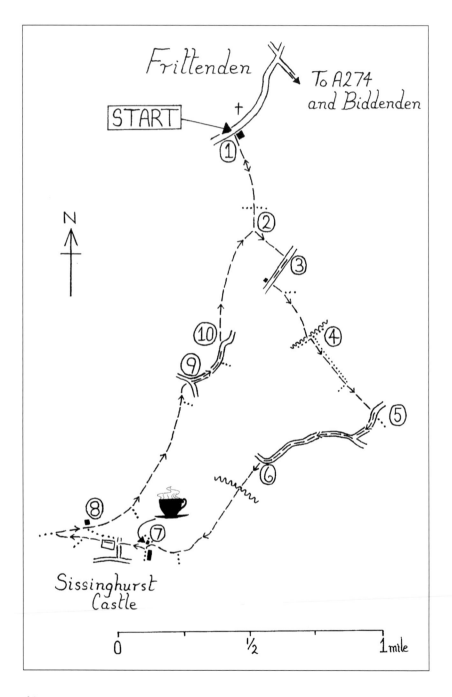

Frittenden

To A274
and Biddenden

START

N

Sissinghurst
Castle

0   ½   1 mile

2. Bear left to a stile and on across another field to a stile onto a lane.

3. Turn right for 190 yards, then left on a signed path that starts along a concrete track opposite Brissenden Farm. Some 20 yards after the concrete finishes, fork right off the obvious track to a stile. Over the stile continue ahead across two fields to a footbridge over a stream.

During the next part of the walk, look right for a view of Sissinghurst Castle. The existing buildings are all that are left of a great Tudor manor house built by the Baker family from Cranbrook. Sir John Baker was a prominent politician in the reigns of Henry VIII, Edward VI and Mary. He served as Attorney General, Chancellor of the Exchequer and Speaker of the House and used his position to advance his wealth. His enthusiasm for persecuting Protestants earned him the sobriquet 'Bloody Baker'. The rector of Frittenden arrested the local miller Edmund Allin and his wife Katherine and brought them to trial as heretics before Baker. Their crime was said to be the sale of corn 'one half cheaper than others'! They were burned at the stake in Maidstone on 18th June 1557.

4. Now follow a path ahead along the left-hand side of a field to a footbridge over a dyke, then continue through a strip of scrub and across a field to a lane.

5. Turn right, then right again at a T-junction. Walk along the lane for about ½ mile.

The fortunes of the Baker family declined in the 17th and 18th centuries. In the 1750s the castle was reduced to holding French prisoners of war. One of the officers guarding them was Edward Gibbon, the historian, who wrote that, 'the duty was hard, the dirt most oppressive'. The prisoners were crammed in and conditions were brutal; they murdered their guards and were killed in reprisal. Sissinghurst was left a wreck and most of the mansion was pulled down about 1800.

6. At a right-hand bend, turn left on a signed bridleway and follow it towards Sissinghurst Castle, seen ahead. Ignore a path on the left as you approach the castle and continue ahead to the teashop on the right, beyond the National Trust shop.

View from the Tower

This decline was arrested in 1930 when Vita Sackville-West and Harold Nicholson bought what remained of Sissinghurst Castle. They restored the Tudor buildings and created the wonderful garden that attracts visitors from all over the world: the White Garden planted entirely with white and grey plants, the walk of pleached limes, the herb garden, the orchard and other 'rooms' leading into each other. The oast house contains an exhibition that describes the story of the estate and the transformation from derelict manor to famous garden. The gardens were first opened to the public in 1938 when to visit cost a shilling. Vita was glad to welcome the 'mild gentlemen and women' and nicknamed them 'shillingses'. The property passed to the National Trust in 1967.

7. Return to the driveway and turn right, passing the ticket office on the right, and follow the signs to the car park. Walk along the right-hand side of the car park and two small fields used as overflow car parks to a stile. Note some cottages to the right. The right of way ultimately leads back past them. Over the stile go ahead, more or less parallel with the right-hand side of the field, to a stile on the right giving on to a track. Turn right to lead back to the front of the cottages noted earlier.

8. Bear left off the track onto a tree-lined path. This eventually becomes a drive that leads to a lane at a junction.

9. Take the lane ahead, signed 'Sandy Lane', for about 300 yards to a stile on the left.

10. Over the stile, bear right past an isolated tree to a second stile and then press on in the same direction, navigating from stile to stile when the path is not visible on the ground. This path leads to a post, passed on the outward route. Turn left, towards Frittenden, and follow the outward route back to the start.

Note: If you started the walk at Sissinghurst, turn right here if you do not wish to visit Frittenden.

Walk 10
OAD STREET

This gentle amble explores the fields and orchards west of Sittingbourne, calling in at a Craft Centre and its excellent teashop along the way. It is easy walking, mostly on the level, with some unexpectedly good views on the return leg.

The teashop at Oad Street Craft Centre serves an irresistible selection of delicious cakes. There are also scones and toasted teacakes. It is worth timing your visit to have lunch. There is an excellent choice of salads or hot dishes such as tasty cauliflower cheese or lasagne. There is also a choice of sandwiches or filled jacket potatoes. It has a large, airy interior decorated in conservatory style and some tables outside in an attractive courtyard. They are open every day except between Christmas and New Year, between 9.30 am and 5.30 pm. Telephone: 01795 843130.

DISTANCE: 3 miles.

MAP: OS Explorer 148 Maidstone and the Medway towns.

HOW TO GET THERE: From the roundabout at the junction of the A2 and A249 take a minor road signed 'Chestnut Street Danaway' for about ¼ mile to a lay-by on the right, just before the first road on the right.

STARTING POINT: Lay-by in Chestnut Street. This is the truncated end of a road obliterated when the A249 was altered. It is almost opposite School Lane (GR 876639).

ALTERNATIVE STARTING POINT: If you wish to visit the teashop at the beginning or end of your walk, start at the Craft Centre at Oad Street. Permission should be sought before leaving a car for an extended period. The teashop is in the Craft Centre. You will then start the walk at point 6.

THE WALK

1. Return to the road and cross it to walk along School Lane for about ¼ mile to a house on the left, just before a right-hand bend in the lane.

2. At the end of the wall round the garden, turn left on a path that climbs through scrub for a few yards before emerging in a field. This path is not obvious; the stone way-mark is on the ground a few feet after the path starts. Go ahead across the field for about 200 yards then turn right on a cross path to a stile. Over the stile go along the left-hand side of a field to a post with way-marks, then strike left across a field in the direction shown by an arrow on the post. At the time of writing this path had not been reinstated. Continue in the same direction as shown by a line of posts with yellow arrows to a track and shortly to a road.

3. Turn left. At a road junction with Pond Farm Road turn right for 250 yards.

This is Borden. The main part of the village lies to the left along Pond Farm Road. The Rat and Sparrow Club started in 1901 and continued until 1960 to destroy pests. They brought rats' tails, sparrows' heads and queen wasps to committee meetings and were paid a reward. Each member had to collect at least 100 sparrows' heads in the year to qualify for the free annual dinner.

4. Take a path on the right, signed with the familiar local stone marker. Head across the field to the left-hand edge of a hedge that

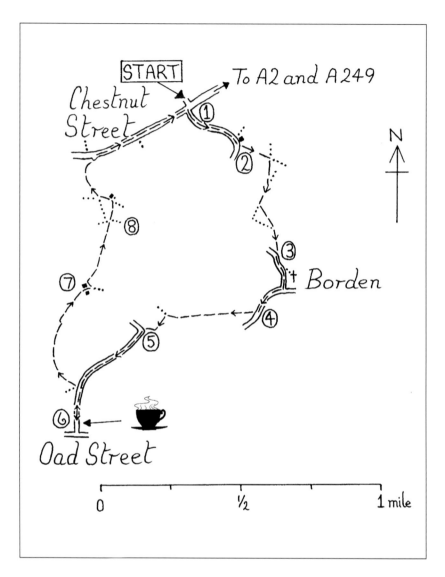

extends half way across the field, to find a gap in the hedge giving on to a hedged path. Follow this for 110 yards to a fork. Bear left. This shortly becomes another hedged path leading to a lane.

☕ **5.** Turn left along the lane for about ½ mile to the Craft Centre and teashop on the left.

6. Turn right out of the Craft Centre and return along the lane for 200 yards to a point where two paths leave the lane on the left. Take the right-hand one of the two paths, along the right-hand side of an orchard, to a double stile onto a fenced path. This leads to a stile. Over the stile turn left for 10 yards then right to continue in the same direction, again on a fenced path.

7. Just after passing between stables turn left over a stile. This leads up to a second stile into a field. Over the stile turn right to a third stile, then bear slightly left to a stile surrounded by holly into woodland. **Do not mistake this for another stile some 40 yards to the left into a field.**

8. Follow the path down through the woods into a yard, then bear left on a surfaced drive that eventually leads down to the road in Chestnut Street. Turn right back to the start.

Walk 11
APPLEDORE

This is a very attractive and varied walk. It starts with a beautiful woodland stretch before dropping down to the Royal Military Canal. A level and easy path takes you by the canal all the way to Appledore and its welcome teashop. The return is across farmland, passing a mysterious mound and an ancient chapel before re-entering the woods to return to the start. Be warned that some paths are nettley in high summer. They are quite passable but shorts would be distinctly uncomfortable.

Appledore Tea Room is a charming traditional tea room housed in a 16th century Grade II listed building. This has had a variety of uses through its long history including a school-room, army hospital and bakery. It is said that Lloyd George once dined here. They serve an excellent selection of delicious home-made cakes and scones. Other teatime goodies are also available and this is one of the few teashops that really does serve crumpets. Sandwiches are offered for a light lunch and they also carry a particularly wide choice of teas. Appledore Tea Room is open Friday to Sunday throughout the year and on Wednesday and Thursday as well between March and October. The opening hours are 10.30 am until 5.30 pm in summer and 11 am until 4 pm in winter. Walkers are welcome, as shown by the unusual boot cleaner outside, but are asked to remove muddy footwear.

When the tea shop is closed there are two pubs and a restaurant in Appledore.

DISTANCE: 6½ miles.

MAP: OS Explorer 125 Romney Marsh, Rye and Winchelsea.

HOW TO GET THERE: From the B2067, Tenterden to Hythe road, at Woodchurch take a road south, signed 'Appledore 3', for 2 miles to Park Wood picnic site on the left.

STARTING POINT: Park Wood picnic site car park (GR 953317).

ALTERNATIVE STARTING POINT: If you wish to visit the teashop at the beginning or end of your walk, start in Appledore village car park behind the Parish Hall. The teashop is right along the main road. You will then start the walk at point 6 or 7.

THE WALK

1. Take a path leading left from the car park. Follow this through the wood, ignoring all paths to left and right and cross a boardwalk after about ¼ mile. Just after this continue ahead at an off-set cross path and carry on wending through the wood to a T-junction with a cross path.

2. Turn right for 10 yards then left on a way-marked path to a lane.

3. Turn right to a road then right again for 160 yards. Turn left through a metal field gate onto a broad, grassy path. This can be overgrown and muddy in places, but press on determinedly to a lane.

4. Turn left.

5. Immediately before a bridge over the Royal Military Canal, turn right. After about 40 yards bear left to walk beside the canal to Appledore. Turn right through the village to the teashop on the left.

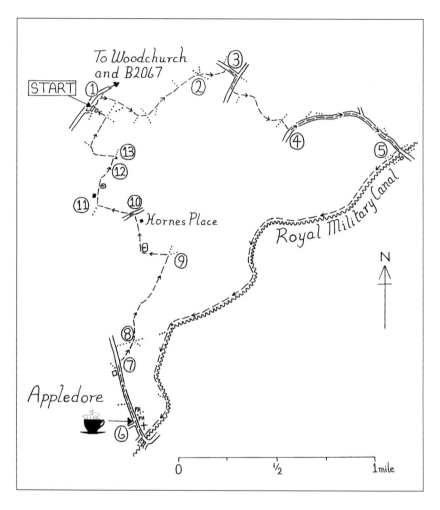

In 1803 the threat of invasion by the French, led by Napoleon Bonaparte, was very real and defences were constructed all along the coast (see walk 19). The Royal Military Canal was part of these. It is a defensive ditch 23 miles long dug by French prisoners of war. Artillery and cavalry would not be able to cross and infantry would have to swim, getting their powder wet. The canal is built in zigzags and there were gun emplacements strategically placed to provide devastating crossfire to mow down the invading forces. At intervals there were sluice gates that could be opened to flood Romney Marsh to further impede an invading army. The canal was finished in 1809 but by that time the threat of invasion had receded and it

The Royal Military Canal

was never used (see walk 16). When Britain was again under threat of invasion in 1940 the 19th century gun emplacements were replaced by their modern equivalent and one of the pillboxes still stands.

6. Turn left out of the teashop and continue walking through the village.

A thousand years ago Romney Marsh was an archipelago of small islands separated by tidal creeks. Appledore stood on a low promontory and Romans and Vikings both used this safe anchorage. For 300 years between about 1100 and 1400 it was a busy port, exporting wool and linen to France and importing wine, silk and other luxury goods. It also had a thriving ship building and repair industry. Appledore was raided by the French in 1380 during the Hundred Years War when they sacked and burned the town. This accounts for some unusual features of the church. When it was rebuilt after the French raid it was designed to provide a refuge and stronghold if the French should come again. The walls are of fortress thickness, the tower was enlarged and the nave and north aisle combined into one to provide a large open space for people to gather. Eventually the Rother estuary silted up and Appledore was cut off from the sea; it now stands more than 8 miles inland. It sank into obscurity and became known as an unhealthy place, damp and riddled with ague, the English name for malaria. The coming of the Royal Military Canal improved communications and the draining of the marsh reduced the threat of disease making Appledore the attractive community it is today, with many fine buildings lining the wide main street.

7. Some 130 yards after the Parish Hall and car park on the left, take a signed path on the right. Head across a recreation ground to a surfaced track and gate in the far corner.

8. Go through the gate and turn left, initially along the left-hand side of a field and then, when the bushes on the left finish, bear right to a stile and bridge in the far right corner. Now head across a field to a stile and on up to and over a mound seen ahead.

This mound is a Bronze Age round barrow. Inside is a small stone chamber used to bury the ashes of one person or perhaps one family. This was then covered with earth. When it was constructed it would have stood looking out over the sea.

9. At the edge of the field turn left to walk in the same field, with a wire fence on the right, down to a stile by a gate. Walk to the left of a small lake and round the far side to a track and on to a lane.

On the right is Hornes Place. The 1380s must have been exciting times to live in Appledore. Not only was there the French raid but in 1381 King Richard II, desperate for money, levied the third poll tax in four years. The ordinary people took the view, 'Can't pay, won't pay' and rose up in revolt throughout Essex and Kent led by Wat Tyler. The people of Appledore burned down the house of the local squire, William Horne, before joining the march on London. The King made all sorts of promises to the rebels to persuade them to disperse. These were soon broken, the leaders executed and throughout the county, including Appledore, there was savage retribution on those who had taken part. Remember the Chinese curse, 'May you live in interesting times!' The chapel attached to the house has been restored, having been used as a barn, and is now in the care of English Heritage and open to the public.

10. Turn left for 35 yards, then right on a broad path. At the time of writing, the first couple of hundred yards, as far as a wire gate on the left, is mown; after that, it is somewhat overgrown, though still easily passable. Press on for about 100 yards to a stile and ahead a few feet to a cross track.

11. Turn right. When the track shortly ends by a house on the left, go ahead over a stile by a gate and across a field to a second stile. Over this bear slightly right, as shown by the way-mark arrows. The path is rather faint as it wends its way between young trees and leads to a third stile over a fence on the right.

12. Over the stile turn left to meet a wire fence. Turn right beside the fence to find a stile. Go over the stile and ahead for 20 yards to meet a cross path on a bend.

13. Turn left. When the path forks, bear right and continue to a cross path. Turn left and this leads back to the car park where this walk started.

Walk 12
CHARING

This walk treads the footsteps of history. Much is along an ancient track-way that has been in use since before the Romans. Once it was a trade route, carrying flint from a factory nearby. A thousand years later, pilgrims used it on their way to Canterbury. Today, it is part of a long-distance recreational path, the North Downs Way. The route also visits the ancient but lively community of Charing – a village today but with the feel of a small town.

The aptly named Pilgrim's Table on the High Street in Charing offers a selection of cakes as well as cream teas and other teatime favourites, such as toasted teacakes. Sandwiches are available for lunch as well as a choice rather different from the average tea room. For example, on my visit there was duck breast with hoi sin sauce followed by roast plums and greengages. In addition to tea, herbal infusions such as camomile and spiced apple are offered. The Pilgrim's Table is decorated in an attractive and unusual medieval style with polished wooden floors and a wood burning stove in an inglenook fireplace. There is an attractive garden at the rear with tables shaded by parasols. They are open between 10 am and 5 pm on Wednesday to Saturday and 2 pm until 6 pm on Sunday throughout the year. They also open in the evening for dinner. Telephone: 01233 712170.

When the tea shop is closed there are several pubs in Charing that serve food, notably the Royal Oak.

DISTANCE: 3 miles, or 4 miles if you begin at the alternative start.

MAP: OS Explorer 137 Ashford, Headcorn, Chilham & Wye.

HOW TO GET THERE: See notes below. Charing is at the junction of the A252 and the A20.

STARTING POINT: The walks in this book are designed to visit the teashop in the second half of the walk. This route is unusual because I think it is better if you start in Charing, where the teashop is located on the High Street, and visit the teashop before or after your walk. There are three car parks: one on Station Road, one on the A20 and one outside the church, off the High Street. The directions start from the High Street in Charing (GR 953494).

ALTERNATIVE STARTING POINT: If you wish to visit the teashop part way round your walk, start at Hart Hill (GR 940505). From the A20, Maidstone-Ashford road, 1 mile west of Charing take a minor road north, signed 'Hart Hill ¼ Stalisfield 2¼', for about ¼ mile to an informal lay-by on the left. Cross the road to a track signed 'By-way' and way-marked with the North Downs Way acorn logo. Walk along it for about ½ mile to pick up the route at point 4.

THE WALK

Charing grew up on the Roman London to Dover road and so has been making a living from looking after travellers for over 2,000 years. Do have a look at the charming High Street; many of the buildings are 16th century or even earlier behind later facades and there are plaques to draw your attention to points of interest. The origin of the market is so lost in history that it never had a charter. A charter to hold two fairs, one on St George's Day in April and the other on St Luke's Day in October, was granted by Henry VI in about 1443. By the 19th century these had become so rowdy that the charter was withdrawn in 1873.

1. Take School Road leading off the High Street.

2. At the roundabout turn right along the A252 for about 250 yards to a stile and signed footpath on the left.

The village of Charing

3. Over the stile, bear slightly left to two gates, then bear slightly right uphill to a stile onto a cross path. At the time of writing, this path is not visible on the ground though a path leading further to the right can be seen.

4. Turn right. (Note: If you began the walk at the alternative starting place, turn left back to the start.) As the main track bends right at a house called 'Twyford', bear left, then bear right at a fork after a further 20 yards to emerge on the A252.

This ancient trackway was old before medieval pilgrims started travelling to Canterbury to visit the shrine of Thomas à Becket. In those days the countryside was much more forested than it is today – and in the forest lurked thieves waiting to prey on unsuspecting travellers. Pilgrims used to gather together in groups for mutual protection. One such group is immortalised in Chaucer's 'Canterbury Tales', an account of the stories they told to entertain themselves on the road.

5. Cross the road and turn left for 20 yards then turn right on a lane, way-marked with the North Downs Way acorn logo. Walk along this quiet lane for ½ mile.

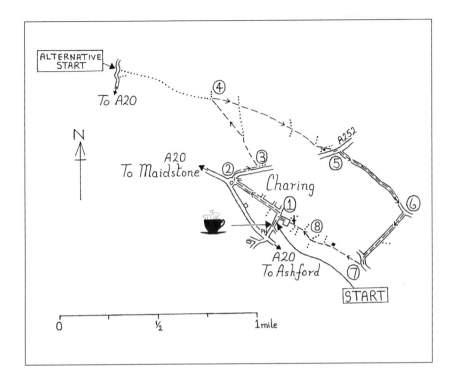

6. Take a lane on the right and follow it to a T-junction. Turn left for 65 yards, then cross a stile on the right by a metal field gate.

7. Bear right in the direction of Charing church to a stile and on across a field. At the far side go through a gap in a hedge and along the left-hand side of a field containing a scout hut. Press on in the same direction along the right-hand side of some playing fields.

8. At the end of the playing fields bear right on a fenced path and follow this into a churchyard. Walk through the churchyard and ahead along a road to the High Street.

Egbert II, King of Kent, gave the lands at Charing to the church at Canterbury in the 8th century and so it remained until the 16th century. Archbishops of Canterbury used to stay at the Manor House, on the right just beyond the church, which became known as the Archbishop's Palace and is now Palace Farm. John Morton, Archbishop at the end of the 15th century probably built much of the present farmhouse, though the great arch is earlier. Archbishop Morton had an irresistible method of raising money for King Henry VII, known as Morton's Fork. If people lived well, that was evidence they were rich whereas if their style was less opulent, they must have substantial savings. Either way, they could afford to contribute plenty to the King's coffers. Henry VIII stopped here in 1520 on his way to meet the French king at the Field of the Cloth of Gold with a retinue of over 4,000. He visited again in 1544 and this time liked it so much that he took it for himself, giving the Archbishop other land in exchange. The present church is basically 13th century, though there was a church on the site much earlier. In 1590 a Mr Dios was shooting birds when the hot shot set fire to the roof. It burned so fiercely that even the bells melted and nothing was left except the walls. The church used to contain a block on which John the Baptist was supposed to have been beheaded, brought back from the Holy Land by Richard the Lionheart. It may have gone up in the conflagration or was perhaps carried off by the Commissioners during the Reformation. The open space on the left is called Clewards Meadow and just beyond it an attractive small garden has been created. This is centred round an unusual human sundial.

Walk 13
PERRY WOOD AND CHILHAM

This is a lovely route that shows the walker the best that Kent has to offer – woodlands, fertile fields and orchards, quiet lanes and tracks and a charming, historic village complete with a teashop. It starts in Perry Wood, one of the most outstanding stretches of woodland in the county, and climbs to a view point before switchbacking across the Downs to join the North Downs Way for the last mile or so into Chilham. Fully refreshed, the return is mainly through orchards and by quiet lanes and more woodland. The climbing involved is amply rewarded by the views and this is a highly recommended route.

 The Copper Kettle is a charming, traditional teashop housed in a 15th century building in a truly enviable position in The Square in Chilham. It has some tables outside where you can watch the world go by in clement weather. It serves a selection of cakes and cream teas and snacks such as soup, pate and French bread or croque monsieur are available all day. Hot lunches are available until 2.30 pm and daily specials are offered. In winter they serve a roast lunch on Sundays. The Copper Kettle is open between 10 am and 5 pm every day in summer, just closing on Monday and Tuesday from November to March. Telephone: 01227 730303.

When the teashop is closed, there are two pubs in Chilham that serve food.

DISTANCE: 7 miles.

MAP: OS Explorer 149 Sittingbourne and Faversham.

HOW TO GET THERE: From the A251 2 miles south of junction 6 of the M2, take a minor road east, signed 'Selling 2 Shottenden 3'. Follow the road for just over 2 miles, through Selling. Turn right on a minor road, signed 'Perry Wood ½ Shottenden 2 Molash 2½'. At a crossroads turn left, signed 'Chilham 2¾' to a car park on the left.

STARTING POINT: Perry Wood car park (GR 045556).

ALTERNATIVE STARTING POINT: If you wish to visit the teashop at the beginning or end of your walk, start in Chilham where there is ample parking in the village car park. The teashop is right out of the car park, in The Square. You will then start the walk at point 7.

THE WALK

Perry Wood is one of the finest areas of woodland in Kent and is owned by Swale District Council to preserve public access. Look out for three magnificent beech trees shortly after the start of the walk. There is a fourth, equally old but now much reduced. Beech is a lovely tree with smooth, grey bark and glossy green leaves. It is especially beautiful in the spring, when the newly emerged leaves are so fresh, and in autumn when they change from gold to orange to brown. Southern England is the northernmost extent of the beech's range: individual trees are found further north but there are no extensive beech woods. The fruit of the beech is a three-sided nut, sometimes called mast, enclosed in a capsule with quite soft prickles on the outside. Fruit in quantity is produced only in irregular so-called mast years, sometimes at quite long intervals. In other years a late spring frost interferes with the setting of the nuts or a cool summer prevents their ripening. This is one reason why oak is the dominant tree in most of Britain. Beech has such a dense canopy that it absorbs a lot of the light and not much can grow beneath it, so the forest beneath beech is very open.

The Pulpit

1. Return to the lane and take a signed bridleway opposite. Follow the main path uphill. Here, admire the three beech tress. When it forks, bear left, shortly crossing a plank bridge across a muddy area. At the next fork, immediately after the entrance to Keeper's Cottage, take the right option, climbing through woodland. Ignore all side paths and press on to the viewpoint where there is also a welcome seat, dedicated to a well-respected local resident.

The viewing platform is called the Pulpit, for obvious reasons. Once there was one of a chain of semaphore signalling stations here. These were established during the Napoleonic War, when there was real fear of invasion. Its main purpose was to transmit intelligence and orders between Deal and London.

2. Pass to the left of the Pulpit and take the path ahead, now steeply downhill. At the bottom of the steep slope turn right on a cross path. As the path begins to bear right after 100 yards, bear left on a smaller, unsigned path that shortly leads to a stile into a field. Over the stile, walk along the left-hand side of a field to a lane.

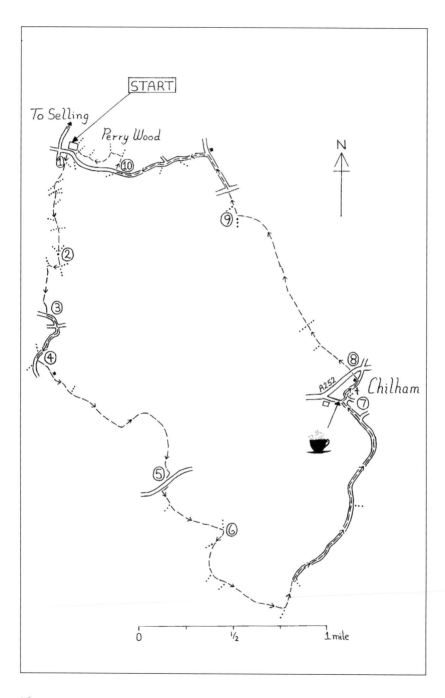

3. Turn left. At crossroads go ahead on a lane, signed 'Denne Manor ¾ No Through Road' for about ¼ mile.

4. Turn left on a surfaced track, signed 'Byway'. Continue on the track when the surface ends at Chequers Farm, for about a mile to a major road.

5. Turn right for 75 yards, then left along the track towards Young Manor Farm: despite the notice saying this is a private road, it is a public footpath. As the track bends right, cross a stile by a gate on the left and head up the right-hand side of two fields. At the top right-hand corner of the second field go ahead a few yards through woods to meet a cross path.

6. Turn right and follow the main path, pausing to admire another magnificent beech to the left of the path. Ignore all side paths and continue ahead when the North Downs Way joins. Go through a gate and carry on down a lane for a mile. Turn left up School Hill into The Square to find the teashop.

Chilham is the quintessential perfect English village, perhaps rather self-consciously so, and it attracts many visitors. Castle and church face each other across The Square with the remaining sides filled with harmonious Tudor and Jacobean buildings. The perfection is marred only by the vehicles parked in The Square, despite the car park close by. The village occupies an easily defensible, hilltop position. The ancient Britons made a stand on the site of the Castle against the invading Roman army in 55 BC, and caused them to retreat, only to return later. The site became a Roman camp, then a Saxon stronghold, a Norman castle and finally a stately home. There has been a church here since Saxon times. The present building dates from the 14th century with, as ever, many later additions. It houses many monuments and it is interesting to see how styles change. There is one to a Lady Palmer, who must have been a paragon for we are told that she was fairer than most women and wiser than most men. Another, from the 19th century, is to two children who died within a few days of each other and shows their toys. The church door is riddled with holes, said to be bullet holes but more likely left by nails used to stick up notices. Do take time to wander round the rest of this lovely village, based on four streets, one from each corner of The Square.

7. Turn left out of the teashop, then left down Church Hill.

The orchards, with Chilham beyond

Immediately after a garage on the left, turn left on a short path that cuts through to the main road. This is easy to miss. If you reach the main road, turn left for 75 yards.

8. Cross the main road to continue in the same direction up the left-hand side of a field to a small gate. Through the gate, press on in the same direction along a broad grassy path through orchards for the best part of a mile. The path then becomes a more obvious track and bends left to meet a surfaced track.

9. Turn right to a lane. Walk up a lane opposite and take the first lane on the left at Little Stonestile Farm for about ½ mile, passing a lane on the right.

10. Turn right through metal barriers opposite a signed bridleway and track. After 135 yards turn left. At a T-junction with a cross path, turn left and at a second T-junction, in front of a wooden fence, turn left again and this leads back to the start.

HASTINGLEIGH AND THE DEVIL'S KNEADING TROUGH

Anyone who does this excellent walk will be in no doubt why this area of Kent has been designated an Area of Outstanding Natural Beauty. There are attractive views throughout and the climax is a walk along the top of the scarp slope of the North Downs with vistas that stretch for miles. Those interested in the natural world will not be disappointed with a fascinating geological feature to inspect and extensive chalk grassland. There is a carpet of flowers in season. Added to all this is an excellent restaurant serving lunches and teas just where you would wish it to be.

 The Devil's Kneading Trough Restaurant was voted the seventh best restaurant in England by the *Financial Times* in 1998 and is a must. It is wonderfully positioned to take advantage of the panoramic views and the modern building has floor to ceiling windows. There are also some tables outside. As this is more of a restaurant than a rural teashop, walkers are asked to remove muddy footwear. They are open every day throughout the year from 10.30 am and serve morning coffee, excellent lunches, as well as teas between 3 pm and 5 pm. There is a good and varied selection of cakes as well as other teatime goodies. Cream teas can include strawberries in season. The choice for lunch ranges from full meals to lighter snacks such as sandwiches and filled jacket potatoes. Telephone: 01233 813212.

DISTANCE: 6 miles.
MAP: OS Explorer 137 Ashford, Headcorn, Chilham and Wye.
HOW TO GET THERE: From the B2068, which runs north from junction 11 of the M20 to Canterbury, 6 miles north of the M20 take a minor road west signed 'Elmsted Hastingleigh Wye'. Ignore all side turns and follow the road to Hastingleigh. Park just before the village hall on the left as you enter the village.
STARTING POINT: Hastingleigh village hall (GR 098449).
ALTERNATIVE STARTING POINT: If you wish to visit the teashop at the beginning or end of your walk, start at the Devil's Kneading Trough where there is ample parking in two public car parks. The teashop is between them. You will then start the walk at point 11.

THE WALK

1. Facing the road, turn left. At the Hastingleigh village sign turn right along a track for 150 yards.

2. Immediately before a wood starts on the left, turn left through a gap in the hedge and walk down the right-hand side of a field. When the wood on the right ends, continue ahead across the field, along the right-hand side of a second field and through a wood to emerge at a junction of lanes.

3. Turn right along the larger of the lanes (not the one with a No Through Road sign) to a T-junction. Go across the road to continue in the same direction on a path signed with a stone way-mark. At the far side of the field is a complicated path junction with two paths to the right and one to the left. Take the second path on the right, heading towards buildings, to find a stile onto a surfaced drive.

4. Turn left. When the surfaced drive ends at a house called 'Little Coombe', continue ahead through a metal gate, initially along the

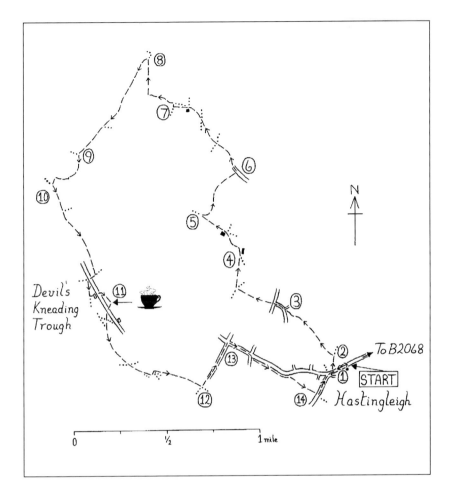

left-hand side of a field and then a hedged path.

5. About 300 yards after 'Little Coombe', watch for a path joining from the right and turn right along it, initially almost back on yourself. (Note: If a gate crosses the path, you have gone about 150 yards too far.)

6. At a lane turn left and press ahead when the lane becomes an unmade track. When the track forks, take the left branch, downhill, to a farm. Now continue uphill on a concrete track to a cross track.

7. Turn right for 20 yards then, immediately before a 'Private' sign, turn left along the left-hand side of a field and follow the path along the edge of a wood.

8. At a T-junction with a cross-track turn left, uphill. Walk through a wood then, more level, beside a field and alongside a second wood to a field gate across the path.

9. Do not go through this. Turn left through a smaller gate to walk along the left-hand side of a field. Skirt left round a second field to a small gate on the left. Go through the gate, turn right and walk round the field to yet another small gate. Go ahead a few yards to a cross-path.

The North Downs are made of chalk laid down millions of years ago at the bottom of the sea. The continents seem immutable to us but, taking a geological time span, they are waltzing around the surface of the globe like a mobile, ill-fitting jigsaw. Some 70 million years ago, the plate on which Africa rides smashed into the plate to the north, crumpling the surface into folds and throwing up the Alps and the chalk hills of southern England. The top of the fold was eroded away, leaving the North and South Downs as a bowl of chalk hills. You are standing on the edge of the bowl some 550 feet above sea level. The views extend to the English Channel and westwards across the valley of the river Stour and Ashford to Ashdown Forest, 40 miles away.

☕ **10.** Turn left. Despite being a national trail, the North Downs Way, the path is surprisingly little worn. Stay close to a fence on the left to meet a drive. Turn right to a road and cross the road to a stile into Wye Downs National Nature Reserve. Over the stile turn left. When the path forks bear left to a car park, road and teashop.

11. Leave the teashop to the left and cross the road to a metal kissing gate. Go ahead and slightly left to meet a cross-path at the very edge of the steep scarp slope. Turn left and follow the sometimes indistinct path over one stile to a second stile and a gate. Go over the stile and follow a fenced path to another stile. Carry on in the same direction along the left-hand side of one field and across a second to a track.

The Devil's Kneading Trough is a steep, dry valley that looks as if a scoop has been taken out of the downs. During the last Ice Age this area was too far south to be covered with sheets of ice. It was an area of tundra, like Alaska today. When the ice melted in warmer periods, the melt-water carved valleys. The steep valley has small terraces on its sides and these show how erosion is continuing today. The last Ice Age may have ended ten thousand years ago but it is only yesterday in geological terms. Given long enough, this erosion will eventually make the valley less and less steep until it is just a shallow depression in the slope, which by then will have itself been further eroded.

As you walk along, pause to look at what is growing around your feet; you will see that it is not just grass but a rich variety of short herbs. In summer when they are in bloom, the sight is a delight. Left to themselves the hills would be covered in oak and beech woods. This typical downland ecosystem is the result of grazing by rabbits and sheep and without the nibbling animals it would quickly revert to scrub and then woods. The animals' teeth nip off any tender, germinating trees or shrubs and prevent them becoming established. There has been a substantial decline in chalk grassland in recent decades. Much has been ploughed up on gentler gradients. On steeper slopes, the threat is from the changed economics of farming that has made sheep rearing less attractive. This area has been made a nature reserve to help conserve the plants and the butterflies and other invertebrates that live on them.

12. Turn left. The track is shortly surfaced: follow it to a lane.

13. Turn right. At crossroads take a signed path on the right, initially parallel with the road along the left-hand side of a field. Towards the end of the field, the path veers right to a gap in a hedge and a couple of stiles. Press on along the left-hand side of two small fields to a lane.

14. Turn left to the main road and turn right back to the start.

Walk 15
LYMBRIDGE GREEN

Starting and finishing in tranquil woodland, this is an exceptionally easy walk. It is almost level and a higher than usual proportion is on well-made tracks and quiet lanes. The woodland stretches are most attractive, with a wide variety of native species growing up among mature planted conifers. The rest of the route passes through pleasant countryside with some good views across a rolling, pastoral landscape.

 The high spot of this walk will undoubtedly be a visit to Oak Tree Farm Tea Rooms. I have rarely enjoyed such a well-stuffed jacket potato served with an interesting and innovative salad. It is a charming, traditional tea room in a modern building. There are tables outside; some shaded by a loggia and others in a pergola covered with honeysuckle. There is an excellent selection of delicious cakes and a number of set teas. These include cream teas, and a Welsh tea with cheese and onion on toast followed by buttered Bara Brith. The children's tea includes a boiled egg with soldiers. Lunch options include sandwiches, which you can have toasted, filled jacket potatoes and daily specials. Oak Tree Farm Tea Rooms are open every day except Monday between noon and 5 pm from the beginning of April until the end of September. In the winter, they are open on Sunday only and close entirely for February. On Sunday throughout the year a very popular roast lunch is served and you must book for this. Teas are served on Sunday from about 3 pm.

DISTANCE: 5 miles.

MAP: OS Explorer 138 Dover, Folkestone and Hythe.

HOW TO GET THERE: From junction 11 of the M20 take the B2068, which runs north to Canterbury. Some 5 miles north of the M20 at Sixmile Garage take a minor road east, signed 'Rhodes Minnis 1½ Lyminge 2¾ for ½ mile to a track on the right. (This is not the track after ¼ mile by a house called 'Forest Lodge'.) Drive down the track a short distance, bearing left, where several parking areas have been created.

STARTING POINT: West Wood parking area (GR 141439).

ALTERNATIVE STARTING POINT: If you wish to visit the teashop at the beginning or end of your walk, start at the teashop, where permission should be sought before leaving a car for an extended period. You will then start the walk at point 7.

THE WALK

1. Return to the road and cross it slightly right to a track. Walk along the track through the woods to a lane.

The varied landscapes of England are nearly all man-made. Without human influence, nearly all of England would be clothed in a mantle of mixed, deciduous forest – the temperate rain forest. Very little, if any, of that primeval forest remains. It has been cleared down the centuries to make way for agriculture and to provide raw materials for building. The lack of wood to shore up trenches was a real difficulty in the First World War. The Forestry Commission was set up in 1919 to create a strategic reserve of timber, and conifers are very quick growing in the warm(!), wet British climate. Trees are a crop that take decades to come to harvest and in that time, the world has moved on. Timber to reinforce trenches is not a priority in the third millennium. The Forestry Commission's role changed to a more commercial one of wood production and then it was privatised so we must now refer to Forest Enterprise. Areas of forest have been allowed to become more mixed because of their landscape and wildlife value.

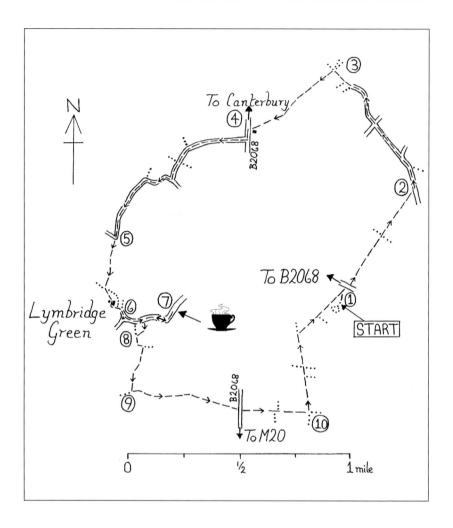

2. Turn left. When the lane bends right, continue in the same direction along a little lane. At a junction with a lane on the right keep ahead. At a fork, take the right branch towards Lower Courthope Farm. When this bends left after 80 yards, carry on in the same direction through a metal field gate for 150 yards.

3. Look for a metal field gate on the left. Do not go through this but cross a stile just beyond it into the next field. Walk along the left-hand side of the field as far as a yellow-topped post. The path now veers diagonally right, heading to the right of some buildings, to a stile onto a drive. Turn right to a road.

4. Turn left for 70 yards then right along a lane signed 'Misling Maxted Street'. Turn right at a T-junction.

5. A bare ½ mile from the T-junction the lane makes a very pronounced right-hand bend. Leave the lane at this point to continue in the same direction along the right-hand side of a field on a signed bridleway. At the end of the field, bear slightly right onto a hedged and fenced path. Stay on the path as it bends left, ignoring paths to right and left, and follow it between buildings and along a drive to a road.

6. Turn left and continue past a timber yard to the teashop on the right.

7. Turn left out of the teashop to return along the road, past the timber yard. Turn left on a signed, fenced path, starting over a stile. Follow the path to a stile onto a track.

8. Turn left for about 100 yards, then cross a stile on the right. Head across a field then along the right-hand side of another field. At the end of a hedge on the right, continue in the same direction across the field.

9. At the far side of the field turn left along a bridleway. At the top of the field follow this into and through a wood to a road. Cross the road and carry on in the same direction through a wood for about ¼ mile to a cross-track, ignoring side paths.

10. Turn left. This track slopes gently downhill. Just before it starts to rise, turn right along a track leading back to the start.

Walk 16
HYTHE

This is a wonderfully diverse route with something for everyone: beautiful woodland footpaths, splendid views and quiet field paths and lanes. The walk is full of historic interest, passing a castle and Roman remains and visiting Hythe for tea. The middle of the walk is beside the Royal Military Canal and the path here is a real delight – grassy, level and most attractive. The path down to the canal can be a bit tricky, as it is steep and sometimes overgrown. However, this can be avoided, if you wish, shortening this longer route by about a mile, albeit missing the best views, Lympne castle, and the Roman remains.

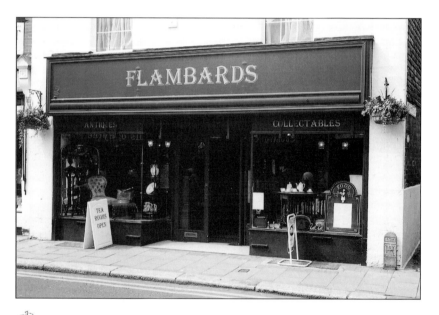

Flambards on the High Street in Hythe shares premises with an antiques shop and examples of stock decorate the walls. This is a traditional and very friendly establishment with a luscious selection of cakes temptingly displayed. Cream teas are served as well as cheese scones and toasted teacakes. For lunch a range of sandwiches with salad is offered or there are filled jacket potatoes and things on toast, including

Welsh Rarebit. Flambards is open Tuesday to Saturday between 10 am and 4.30 pm throughout the year. Telephone: 01303 262889.

When the teashop is closed, there are many pubs, teashops and eating establishments of all sorts in Hythe.

DISTANCE: 8 miles.

MAP: OS Explorer 138 Dover, Folkestone and Hythe.

HOW TO GET THERE: From junction 11 of the M20 take the A20 towards Folkestone. The road is also signed to Brockhill Country Park. After about ½ mile, turn right, signed 'Saltwood' and follow this road for about a mile to the entrance to Brockhill Country Park on the right.

STARTING POINT: Brockhill Country Park car park (GR 148360).

ALTERNATIVE STARTING POINT: If you wish to visit the teashop at the beginning or end of your walk, start in Hythe where there is ample parking in several signed car parks. The teashop is on the High Street. You will then start the walk at point 9.

THE WALK

1. Walk to where the exit drive leaves the car park to find a way-marked path on the left that leads to a road. Turn left.

2. As the road bends right, just after a half-timbered house, turn left on a signed path through a small gate to shortly walk up the right-hand side of a field and then through a wood. Continue ahead as a path joins from the right to eventually reach a small gate into a field. Head across the field to a stile by a gate, to pass in front of a small church and along a track to a road.

3. Turn left for 30 yards then right along a track, passing a pond. When the track bends left, continue ahead through a small gate into a field. Cross the field to another small gate back onto the track. Turn right and follow this to meet a cross-track. Go across this then bear slightly right across a field, heading for the edge of a wood, then on across a second field to two stiles onto a road.

4. Turn right. Pass a lane on the left and a closed lane on the right.

Note: To shorten the walk by about a mile and avoid a tricky, steep downhill path turn left along the lane to the Royal Military Canal and turn left beside it to pick up the route at the car park mentioned in point 7.

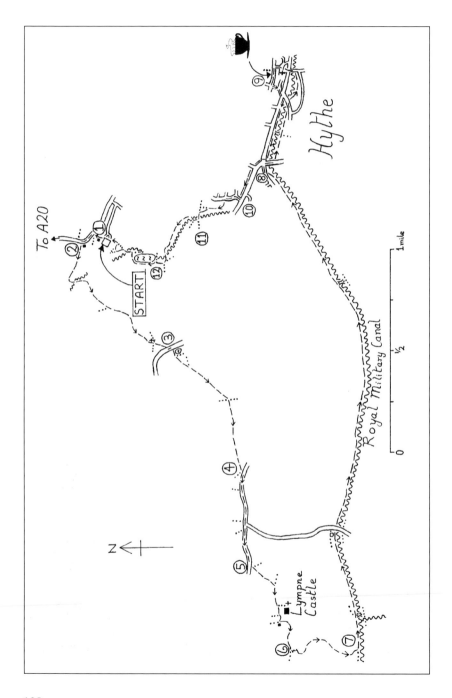

The cross at the junction marks the site of the Court of Shepway where the authorities of the Cinque Ports used to meet. The name comes from 'Shipway' because in centuries past, before it silted up and disappeared, boats used to come up a branch of the river Rother to West Hythe and, in Roman times, to Lympne. This part of the route follows the Saxon Shore Way, a long-distance path that traces the shoreline of Kent as it was perhaps a thousand years ago.

5. As you enter Lympne turn left on a bridleway along a surfaced drive. In front of an arched entrance to Lympne Castle turn right. As the drive bends right in front of a house, turn left along a signed path, which shortly goes along the top of a steep slope.

Lympne is pronounced Lim. The castle was built in the 14th century on the site of earlier buildings and was virtually a ruin at the beginning of the 20th century before it was restored. There are supposed to be several ghosts haunting the castle, including a Roman soldier patrolling the ramparts. When there are stories of ghosts, it is usually a sign to look for some nefarious goings-on in the vicinity. In this case it was smuggling. When an old pew was removed from the church, a chamber was revealed that had been used as a hiding place for contraband. The ghost stories were put

The 19th century Lympne Castle

about to deter unwelcome interest in bumps in the night.

6. Some 15 yards after a wire fence on the left finishes, at a stone footpath sign on the right, bear left off the main path on a steep path that zigzags down the slope to the Royal Military Canal. It is easy to miss this junction.

To the left of the path you can see the remaining fragments of a Roman fort, Portus Lemanus, built in the third century to protect the port, as it was then, of Lympne. The Saxons called it 'stout wale', a description that became the name Stutfall Castle. It was originally higher up the cliff and ended up half way down due to a landslip. These cliffs can be treacherous. The story is told of a house half a mile west that once stood on top of the cliffs. It was called French House because France could be seen from its windows. In 1726 it slipped 50 feet down the cliff but so gently that the occupants knew nothing of their journey until they awoke next morning.

7. Turn left beside the canal and follow it into Hythe, crossing a car park and lane after ½ mile.

The Royal Military Canal was part of the defences against a possible invasion by Napoleon (see walk 11). When Cobbett visited the area in 1823, when Napoleon was no longer a threat, he was scathing about the response to the danger. He wrote, '. . . those armies that had so often crossed the Rhine and the Danube, were to be kept back by a canal, made by Pitt, thirty feet wide at the most.'

8. When the path joins a road in Hythe, continue in the same direction. At a main road turn right over the canal, then left to continue beside it. When the path joins a road, turn left then right on a path by The Duke's Head to carry on by the canal as far as the next bridge. Cross the bridge and a road and walk up by the Methodist church to the High Street. Turn left along the High Street to the teashop on the right.

Until the reign of Henry VIII there was no Royal Navy; the Crown hired ships when it needed them for war or transport. The Cinque Ports were a group of south coast ports that banded together for mutual aid and protection and were granted special privileges in return for supplying ships when needed. Hythe was one of the original Cinque Ports. The estuary has silted up and Hythe is cut off from the sea by a shingle beach, with no trace of the harbour remaining. The long, winding High Street has an 18th century town hall on columns. Nearby is a notice asking everyone, '. . . to unite in their Endeavours to keep this place clean and to prevent Boys or others from dirting [sic] the same.' Francis Pettit-Smith was born at 31 The High Street. He was a farmer who also experimented with new ideas in ships' propulsion. He invented the screw propeller, patenting his idea in 1836. His invention was taken up by the Navy and the great engineer, Isambard Kingdom Brunel, who changed the design of the 'Great Britain' from paddle to screw propulsion.

9. Turn right out of the teashop and follow the High Street as it bends round to the left. At the end of the High Street turn right. Cross the road to a footway, now walking with the Royal Military Canal on the left. At a T-junction turn right then fork left at the next junction along London Road, signed 'M20 Channel Tnl Dover A261 Lympne'.

10. Turn right along Turnpike Hill. Some 70 yards after the last house on the left, turn left off the road on a signed path. Follow this across a grassy area and pick up a path bearing right beside a stream through woods. At a fork bear left to stay by the stream.

11. Shortly after crossing a bridge over the stream go over a stile on the right. Over the stile, follow a path to the right back across the stream, then bear left to keep the stream on your left to another bridge. Cross this and continue upstream, now with the stream on your right, to arrive at a path in front of a small lake.

12. Turn left round the lake. At the end of the lake turn left. This path winds its way back to the car park.

Walk 17
ELHAM

This walk is not long, but it is quite energetic. The route starts in Elham, a most attractive village with several historic buildings, in the valley of the Nail Bourne. It climbs steadily up the side of the valley, mainly on an ancient trackway. Climbing usually rewards the walker with views and this route is no exception. The path then returns to the valley for a well-earned tea before a short stroll back to Elham completes an attractive expedition.

The Shepherd's Hut at Parsonage Farm Rural Heritage Centre serves a selection of cakes and delicious home-made tea-breads. For lunch there is an excellent choice of full meals, including vegetarian options, and lighter snacks including sandwiches and filled jacket potatoes. These are complemented by tempting puddings such as Kentish Bramley apple pudding. As well as the traditional interior there are several tables outside, some under cover, where you can take tea watched by some of the livestock. They are open from early April until the end of September every day except Monday (open Bank Holiday Mondays) from 10.30 am until 5 pm. Telephone: 01303 840356.

When the teashop is closed, there are two pubs in Elham, both serving food.

DISTANCE: 3½ miles.

MAP: OS Explorer 138 Dover, Folkestone and Hythe.

HOW TO GET THERE: From junction 11 of the M20 take the A20 eastbound for about 1 mile to a roundabout. Take a minor road north for about 5 miles through Lyminge to Elham. The Square lies off the main road through the village to the right.

STARTING POINT: The Square, Elham, in front of St Mary's church (GR 177438).

ALTERNATIVE STARTING POINT: If you wish to visit the teashop at the beginning or end of your walk, start at Parsonage Farm Rural Heritage Centre, though permission must be sought before leaving a car for a long period. The teashop is by the car park. You will then start the walk at point 10.

THE WALK

This favoured spot has been inhabited since Neolithic times. The name is pronounced 'Eelham' and it has been suggested that eels were once caught in the Nail Bourne, though this is unlikely in such a small and intermittent stream. It is much more likely that it is named after a Saxon called Ula since it is referred to as Ulaham in a charter dated AD 855. The massive church is mainly 13th century and a guide is available within. The King's Arms is a medieval building but the timbers are hidden beneath a more modern tile-hung façade.

1. With your back to the gates into the churchyard, cross The Square diagonally left. Walk up a lane to return to the main road. Cross the road and carry on up the lane to a T-junction. Turn left for 60 yards then right up Cullins Hill.

There are many fine buildings in Elham including medieval timbered houses and elegant homes built in the 18th century. The heavily timbered Abbot's Fireside restaurant was built in the 15th century as an inn. The beam-ends below the eaves are carved into grotesque figures. The Duke of Wellington used it as his East Kent headquarters during the Napoleonic Wars. Across the road is the Rose and Crown, which was a coaching inn and features in the adventures of the Scarlet Pimpernel as he travelled between London and Paris.

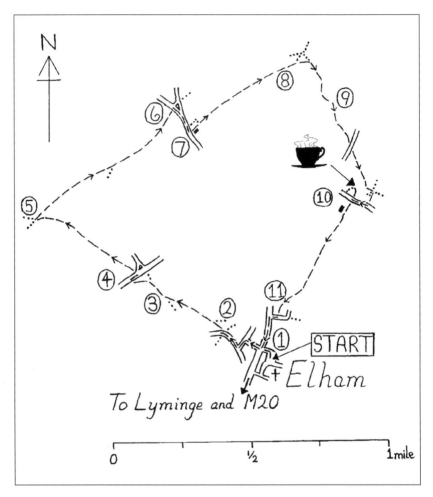

2. At the top of the hill take the second of two paths on the right. The correct path starts along a short surfaced section leading to a stile and, at the time of writing, is the less obviously signed of the two. Over the stile bear slightly left to a second stile and on to meet a cross-path at the far side of the field.

3. Turn right up a sunken, hedged path to eventually emerge on a lane.

4. Turn right for 50 yards, then left over a stile on a signed path.

The path is not visible on the ground at the time of writing but passes along the left-hand side of two fields and the right-hand side of two more to a stile onto a track. The stile is 40 yards to the left of the right-hand corner of the fourth field.

5. Turn right along the track and follow it to a lane.

6. Turn right then right again at a junction.

7. Take a signed path on the left that starts through a field gate next to a white house. The path crosses the garden to a stile then continues along the left-hand side of two fields with a superb view ahead.

8. Go over a stile by a gate. Continue ahead for a few yards. Do not bear left down to a track. Instead, bear right and up to find a stile. There is no obvious path and you have to pick your way along and up the steep slope. Over the stile, bear slightly right to meet a fence. Walk with the fence on the right to a stile.

9. Over the stile, walk along the left-hand side of a field. When the fence on the left ends, look for a green finger post across the field to the left. Walk over to it to find a gate onto a road. Cross the road to a stile then bear diagonally right to a gate. Go through the gate and continue in the same direction for 40 yards. You are now in the grounds of Parsonage Farm Rural Heritage Centre. Please do not leave the public footpath unless paying to visit the Centre. Turn left between fences for another 40 yards to a gate ahead. Go through the gate and turn right to a stile onto a lane. Turn right, then right into the Heritage Centre and the teashop.

Parsonage Farm Heritage Centre is based on a working farm that has been in the Palmer family for over a hundred years. Part of the farmhouse is medieval and old, rare breeds of farm animals are kept. There are displays of old farm machinery and techniques.

10. Return to the entrance and cross the lane to a track. Walk along the track. When the track fades out after some barns on the right, cross a stile by a gate on the left. Walk along the right-hand side of two fields and across a third. Go ahead along a track to a road.

The Nail Bourne is an intermittent stream; it can flow freely in the driest of years and dry up in wet years! It is said that soon after St Augustine's arrival there was a drought in the valley and the Christians were blamed. The saint knelt in prayer and a stream gushed forth and watered the valley. This was too much for the old gods: they summoned up a storm, uprooting trees to block the stream and opening the earth to swallow the waters. Once every seven years the stream escapes and flows again. The word 'bourne' is an old term for a stream.

11. Turn right to the main road. Turn left through Elham. Turn left along St Mary's Road back to The Square and the start.

Walk 18
RECULVER

The twin high spots of this walk are undoubtedly the ruins at Reculver and the return along the cliffs with the sea on the right and flower-filled meadows on the left. The outward leg has features of interest too. It passes a point that would have been high on the shore two thousand years ago, overlooking the Watsum Channel. The Channel has long since silted up but there are remarkably extensive views for a few feet of ascent.

The Snack Bar at Reculver is by no means a traditional teashop. It is more accurately described as a 'sea-side caff', but it does serve an excellent and very reasonably priced mug of tea to refresh you before embarking on a tour of the ruins and the second half of this walk. No cakes – but various traditional puddings with custard are offered and otherwise it is chips with everything. It is most unusually decorated with Coca-Cola wallpaper and has some tables outside. It is open from 10 am at weekends from early March to the end of October and every day during the school holidays. There is no telephone.

When the Snack Bar is closed the pub in Reculver, the King Ethelbert Inn, serves food.

DISTANCE: 4 miles.
MAP: OS Explorer 150 Canterbury and the Isle of Thanet.
HOW TO GET THERE: From the A299, Canterbury to Margate road, 2 miles east of the Herne Bay exit (the A299) take a minor road signed 'Hillborough Reculver Hoath Chislet'. At Hillborough turn left on Reculver Road for ¼ mile then take Bishopstone Lane on the right to a car park.
STARTING POINT: Bishopstone car park (GR 211687).
ALTERNATIVE STARTING POINT: If you wish to visit the teashop at the beginning or end of your walk, start in Reculver where there is ample parking in a large public car park. The teashop is passed on the right as you drive to the car park. You will then start the walk at point 7.

THE WALK

1. Walk back along the lane for 80 yards. Opposite Manor Close cross a stile on the left onto a path across a field, to emerge on a road at a junction.

2. Turn left along Reculver Lane. Immediately after a church on the right, turn right through a small parking area to pick up a path across two fields to find a bridge over a stream. At the time of writing, the bridge is hidden by voracious ivy growing on a fallen tree, but it is passable once you have found it. Over the bridge, follow the path up to the railway.

The church was built in the 19th century but much of its fabric is far older than that, having come from the church at Reculver when it was demolished.

3. Do not take the obvious path over a stile and across the railway. Instead, turn left to soon pick up a track passing to the left of a house and eventually leading to a lane.

4. Turn right as far as a windmill with no sails and a house on the left.

Stood on this spot two thousand years ago you would have surveyed a very different scene. You would have been on the shore looking out over a landscape of tidal marshes and mud flats between one and three miles

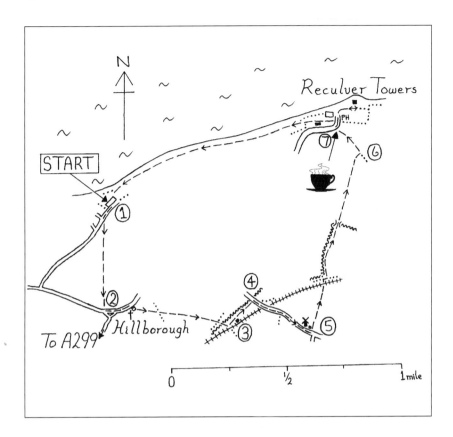

N

~

~

~

Reculver Towers

~

~

~

PH

START

~

①

⑦

⑥

②

④

To A299 Hillborough

③

⑤

0   ½   1 mile

wide with a navigable channel winding through it used by merchantmen and warships. Thanet really was an island in those days, separated from the mainland by Watsum Channel. Down the centuries, the channel silted up until now it is an area of low-lying agricultural land, criss-crossed by drainage ditches.

5. Turn left along a surfaced track. At a cross-track turn right for 30 yards, then left along the left-hand side of two fields and ahead to a track.

When Watsum Channel was open, this path would have been on the sea bed or perhaps struggling along cloying tidal mud flats. As the years pass, more and more silt is deposited on the flats and this raises the level. They are colonised by plants, which in turn trap more silt and the mud flats extend out, eventually choking off the channel. Watsum Channel had

Reculver Towers

ceased to be navigable by the late Middle Ages. This is a common phenomenon and many harbours and shipping lanes are only kept open by dredging. Where this is not done, a seaway that once carried merchantmen and warships turns into fields.

 6. Turn left to the teashop on the left at a junction with a road.

7. Turn right along the road, then bear right to Reculver Towers. After exploring the ruins, return to the road and take a path to the left of the car park. Pass by the Information Centre and follow the path along the cliffs back to the start.

The Romans built a fort here, Regulbium, to guard the important shipping lane of Watsum Channel. It was partnered by another at Richborough to defend the southern end. At that time, Reculver fort was more than a mile inland and it had the usual complement of baths, temples, barracks and civil settlement. The name Reculver means 'great headland' and is an unusual example of a name surviving unchanged from Romano-British times. The sea has eroded the land here at the rate of about a yard a year since then and more than half the fort has been washed away. When the Roman authority collapsed at the end of the 4th century, the fort fell into disuse. A church was built within the site during the 7th century. This was extended and enlarged down the centuries and the prominent towers were built in the 12th century. As the sea advanced and the population moved away, the church became ruinous. It was decided to move the parish church and a new one was built, passed earlier in the walk. When the scheme was mooted, the bishop gave permission providing a majority of local people supported the plan. It only gained approval by the narrowest of margins. Apparently, one of the main movers was the then incumbent's mother who objected to visitors coming to view the romantic ruins. The twin towers were an important landmark. They were bought by Trinity House, the body responsible for safeguarding navigation round Britain's shores, and repaired. Originally, they were topped by wooden spires but these blew down in 1818.

Walk 19
FOLKESTONE WARREN

This is a highly recommended walk exploring an unusual and interesting area. It is certainly the most strenuous walk in this book, though it is by no means the longest. It starts gently enough along the shore, made easy by coastal defences. It makes a welcome change to be able to walk so close to the sea without ploughing through soft sand or shingle. Close to the start is a wave-cut platform, an excellent place for rock-pooling. It is a good idea to time the start of this walk at low water if you want to spend some time investigating the fascinating world of the rocky shore. In addition, a short stretch of beach has to be crossed. This should be passable at all but the highest tides, but is easier at low water. After this pipe-opener along the shore comes the strenuous part – a 400 feet climb up the cliffs. The path is very well constructed and zigzags up, but it is, nonetheless, quite a climb. The teashop is at the point where the path emerges on the cliff top – and it could not be more welcome. The return is along the cliffs with outstanding views before a steep but straightforward descent back to the start.

The Cliff Top Café is perched in a wonderful position on top of the cliffs with outstanding views. It offers a very good selection of cakes as well as cream teas. For lunch there are sandwiches and burgers or hot dogs. There are a couple of tables indoors for less clement weather as well as several outside, shaded by parasols. It is open every day from the beginning of April until the end of October between 10 am and 6 pm. Telephone: 01303 850689.

When the teashop is closed East Cliff Pavilion at the start of the walk serves refreshment of all sorts. In addition, there is a pub that serves food just off the route at point 7.

DISTANCE: 4 miles.

MAP: OS Explorer 138 Dover, Folkestone and Hythe.

HOW TO GET THERE: From junction 13 on the M20 take the A259, signed 'Folkestone Harbour'. Go straight ahead over two roundabouts and you should be on the A260, still signed to the harbour and Country Park. Take the second exit at the next roundabout. This is Wear Bay Road. Follow it to a car park on the left, just before the road reaches the sea.

STARTING POINT: Public car park next to East Cliff Pavilion, Folkestone (GR 239364).

ALTERNATIVE STARTING POINT: If you wish to visit the teashop at the beginning or end of your walk, start in Capel le Ferne where the teashop is to be found on Old Dover Road. There is street parking nearby. You will then start the walk at point 6.

THE WALK

1. Turn left out of the car park and walk in front of East Cliff Pavilion. Take a track by the side of the building. Just before this finishes, turn left up some steps and walk to a Martello Tower.

In 1803 Britain was under threat of invasion by France, led by Napoleon Bonaparte. The obvious invasion route was the short sea crossing from Calais. Napoleon had assembled a force of 130,000 men and gathered a fleet of boats and barges capable of transporting that army to any of several landing sites. The first line of defence was the might of the British Navy but there was always the danger that the French fleet would be able to secure the Channel for the few hours needed for the invasion force to cross. Part of the solution was a line of 103 towers. They were called Martello Towers after a tower at Mortella on Corsica. Occupied by pirates, this had held out for two days against the Royal Navy so the value of the structure was impressed on the authorities. They were cheap and quick to

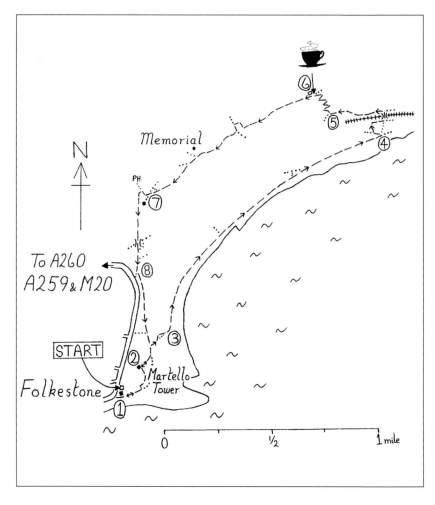

build and stood 33 feet high with walls tapering from 13 feet thick at the base to six feet at the top. The towers were designed to be garrisoned by 24 men. The slit windows would allow the shore to be raked by musket fire while a gun on top could fire a 24 pound cannon ball 1,000 yards to devastate landing craft or could spray the beach with grape shot against infantry. Where the threat was greatest, as here at Folkestone, they were built close together to provide an interlocking field of fire. The defeat of Napoleon at Trafalgar meant they were never used in battle. Many fell into disrepair and some were put to other uses, including target practice for the Navy. In 1940 those that remained were brought into commission once

A view of the cliffs from the route

more against the threatened German invasion. This Martello Tower is used as a seasonal Visitor Centre, open from June until the end of September (admission charge). Telephone: 01303 242113.

2. From the Tower walk right to meet a track to the right of some tennis courts and bowling greens. Turn left along the track for about 50 yards, then turn right on a path signed 'Seashore Trail' down to the beach.

The organisms that live on a rocky shore such as this have to survive in an incredibly difficult environment. They are alternately exposed to desiccation when the tide is out and then are covered with water. They are basically sea animals adapted to life in salt water but are flooded with fresh water when it rains. When the tide is in, creatures from the sea, such as crabs eat them, and when the tide is out they are the prey of sea birds. This is why so many of the animals have a protective shell. The plants are also vulnerable to desiccation when the tide is out and that is why they are so slimy and tough.

117

3. Cross the beach to some concrete sea defences and walk along them for just over a mile, as far as a second wide plinth.

The towering chalk cliffs sit on a layer of much softer clay. This is easily eroded by the waves beating on the shore, leaving the cliffs above with inadequate support so they come tumbling down and form an undercliff. The shingle beach had afforded some protection to this part of the shore. The shingle has always drifted eastwards under the influence of tides and wind. This was interrupted by the development of Folkestone harbour in the 19th and 20th centuries. The shingle in front of the cliff continued to drift east but the supply to replace it was reduced by the harbour, leaving the cliffs less protected. Huge landslips, particularly in 1915, created the undercliff, known as Folkestone Warren. The massive and costly sea defences were built after this.

4. Towards the end of this plinth take a track on the left. Some 25 yards after a metal barrier, opposite a seat, turn right up steps and follow a path to a bridge across the railway. Over the railway, follow the path to the left. This shortly enters a wooded area.

Pictures of the Warren from 70 years ago or so show it to be open and grassy, grazed by sheep, cattle and even semi-wild goats. Changes in agriculture have reduced the amount of grazing and now only small patches of open grass remain. The rest has been invaded by scrub that is being replaced by woodland. This provides a home for a profusion of insects and birds. For example, 330 species of moth live here and 50 species of nesting birds have been recorded.

5. At a fork by a way-mark post bear right on a path that zigzags up the cliff to the teashop on the top.

As you climb the cliffs you might like to ponder the fact that each centimetre took 1,000 years to form as the skeletons of minute sea organisms were deposited on the floor of a warm and shallow tropical sea some 140 million years ago.

6. Go a few yards along the path in front of the teashop into the customers' car park to pick up a cliff-top path. At a track turn left for 40 yards then right to continue on the cliff path. Pass to the left of the Battle of Britain Memorial then bear left to walk closer to the cliff edge for the best views.

The Battle of Britain Memorial, a statue of a young pilot gazing out to sea, is decorated with the crests of the 66 RAF squadrons that fought in the battle. It was opened by the Queen Mother in 1993. It stands on the site of a gun emplacement from where 16 inch guns shelled France.

7. At a cross-path bear right down into a small dip. This point is easy to miss. If you find yourself on the roof of a look-out station, you have gone about 50 yards too far. At the bottom of the dip turn left on an unsigned path. (If you wish to visit the pub, continue ahead for a couple of hundred yards to the road and the Valiant Sailor.) Follow this downhill, crossing a bridge over one surfaced track to a second surfaced track. Turn right along the track.

8. As the track approaches a road, go through a wooden barrier on the left to walk along a grassy area used as a car park and picnic area in summer. Skirt to the left of bowling greens and tennis courts to retrace your steps back to the start.

Walk 20
ST MARGARET'S AT CLIFFE

This walk explores a landscape that has become an icon of nationality – the White Cliffs of Dover. Much of the route is along the top of the cliffs, often with a carpet of chalk flowers at your feet in season. Cliff walks are never level, and this is no exception. However, there are plenty of seats well placed to enjoy the excellent views on the main uphill stretch.

The Blue Bird Tea Rooms enjoy a superb position on the White Cliffs not far from Dover. The theme is wonderfully sustained – but not as far as rationing! In connection with the theme of this book, have a look at the picture on the front of the menu. The food is outstanding. The cakes are delicious and if you can resist them, a cream tea is tempting. The afternoon tea combines the best of both with both scones and cake. For lunch a choice of Country Platters is offered with interesting combinations such as turkey and mango or salmon and dill. They also serve interesting sandwiches, such as creamy mushroom with bacon and sausage. The building that houses the Tea Rooms was once a radar station. When this use ceased it fell into disrepair but was restored and makes a most attractive refreshment break, heated by a wood burning stove in winter. The Blue Bird Tea Rooms are open all year every day except Monday and Friday between 10.30 am and 4.30 pm. Telephone: 01304 853520.

When the tea shop is closed there is a tea room at The Pines passed at point 7. Alternatively, there are several pubs in St Margaret's village.

DISTANCE: 4 miles.
MAP: OS Explorer 138 Dover, Folkestone and Hythe.
HOW TO GET THERE: St Margaret's lies east of the A258, Dover Deal road, and is signed from this road. The car park is in the centre of the village on the right, just after the Clyffe Inn.
STARTING POINT: St Margaret's at Cliffe village car park in Reach Road (GR 358447).
ALTERNATIVE STARTING POINT: If you wish to visit the teashop at the beginning or end of your walk, start at the car park at the Dover Patrol Memorial. The teashop is at the side of the car park. You will then start the walk at point 10.

THE WALK

1. Leave the car park by the road at the rear and follow it round to a main road. Turn right for 125 yards, then turn left along Reach Close to a T-junction. Turn right for just over 100 yards.

2. Turn left on a path across a field to the far right corner. Take the left-hand path gently uphill to a surfaced track.

3. Turn right. When the track reaches a gate signed 'Wanstone Farm Private', turn left on a signed footpath along a track leading towards a lighthouse.

Just offshore are the Goodwin Sands, a vast shifting sandbank that is submerged most of the time and an obvious danger to shipping. It is estimated that over 50,000 lives have been lost in wrecks on the Sands in the last 300 years. There has been a light on the cliffs to warn of the danger since the Middle Ages. Occasionally, the Goodwin Sands are temporarily exposed and have been the venue for some unusual games of cricket. The first recorded match took place on 31 August 1813 between four-man teams from Ramsgate and Bethsden; the latter won by 22 runs to 21.

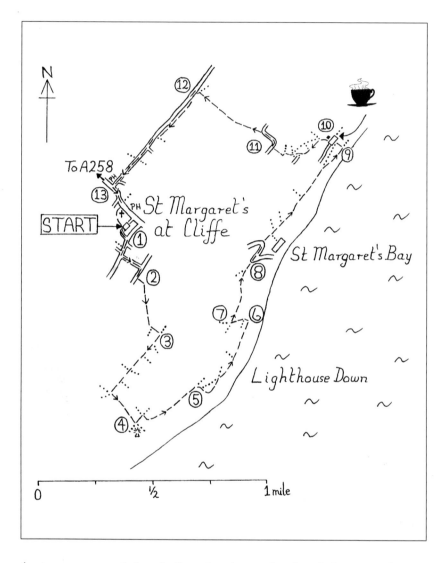

4. At a cross-track just before South Foreland Lighthouse, where a metal gate bars the way right, turn left. At a T-junction with a cross-track turn right.

5. Some 20 yards after a National Trust sign for Lighthouse Down, where a tall, wooden fence on the right finishes, turn right through a gate and follow any of several paths along the cliffs.

6. When a wire fence bars the way ahead, turn left to a gate onto a track. Go ahead in the same direction.

7. At a cross-track turn right for about ¼ mile to emerge on a road at a bend.

The six-acre gardens of the Pines are most attractive and contain a statue of Sir Winston Churchill, unveiled by the wartime leader's grandson, also Winston Churchill, in 1972. One of the big guns positioned near here was nicknamed 'Winnie' and another was, inevitably, called 'Pooh' The story goes that after Winnie was fired for the first time in World War II, the commander called Winston Churchill to report a direct hit. 'On what?' was the query. Back came the answer, 'On France, Sir'. Across the road is a local museum and the tea room, dedicated to Noel Coward, is an alternative refreshment stop. The gardens are open to the public throughout the year and the museum and tea room are open from the end of May until early September. Telephone: 01304 852764.

8. Bear left along the road. When it bends left, turn right on a signed path that shortly leads along the cliffs. There are several seats well positioned to enjoy the views of the White Cliffs. Continue along the cliffs, ignoring all left turns, until you are level with a stone obelisk on top of the cliffs.

St Margaret's Bay, down the road to the right, is a famous suntrap and the closest point to France. It is the traditional departure point for cross-Channel swimmers. Local tradition says it was a notorious haunt of smugglers and the Parish Clerk kept the ropes for hauling contraband up the cliffs in the church tower. In 1865 the then Warden of the Cinque Ports, Lord Granville, decided that the little fishing village should become an up-market seaside resort and the land behind the Bay was laid out for fine residences. The plan never really matured but this attractive spot has attracted its fair share of famous visitors such as Henry Royce (of car fame) and Noel Coward.

9. Turn left up to a wooden kissing gate into a car park and the teashop to the right.

The monument is dedicated to the men of the Dover Patrol, which kept the supply line to France open during the First World War. Despite the enormous sums spent on the Royal Navy in the period before the outbreak

The cliff-top path

of war, insufficient provision had been made for this dangerous task and it was carried out by a scratch force of small ships. Over 1,507 mines were destroyed and more than 2,000 men lost their lives. A similar monument stands on the opposite side of the Channel and can be seen on a clear day.

10. From the teashop walk past the Dover Memorial to a gate on the right immediately beyond it. Through the gate take the path ahead. Just before a gate onto a road, bear right to shortly join a path coming in from the right. Follow this round to the right to a small gate onto a fenced path. Follow this to a lane.

11. Turn right. As the lane bends right to Bockhill Farm, continue in the same direction on a signed path. This leads down into a valley and up the other side to a track. Turn left to shortly meet a lane.

12. Turn left. After 60 yards you can bear left onto a parallel path to reduce road walking; it rejoins the lane just before you enter the village.

13. At the Red Lion turn left. Turn right into the churchyard and follow a path through the churchyard to a gate and a short path that leads back to the car park.

St Margaret's at Cliffe takes its name from its Norman church, dedicated to St Margaret of Antioch. As well as the many old features of interest, there is a modern stained glass window dedicated to three local crew members on the Herald of Free Enterprise who lost their lives when the ship capsized at Zeebrugge. The church rings a curfew bell every night in winter months between Michaelmas (29 September) and Lady Day (25 March) to warn travellers of the dangerous cliff edge. A local man fell over the cliff in 1696 and was fatally injured but survived long enough to bequeath land to pay for this service, which survives to this day.